Machine Knitting Techniques

Lace and Open Fabrics

Elena Berenghean

Machine Knitting Techniques

Lace and Open Fabrics

THE CROWOOD PRESS

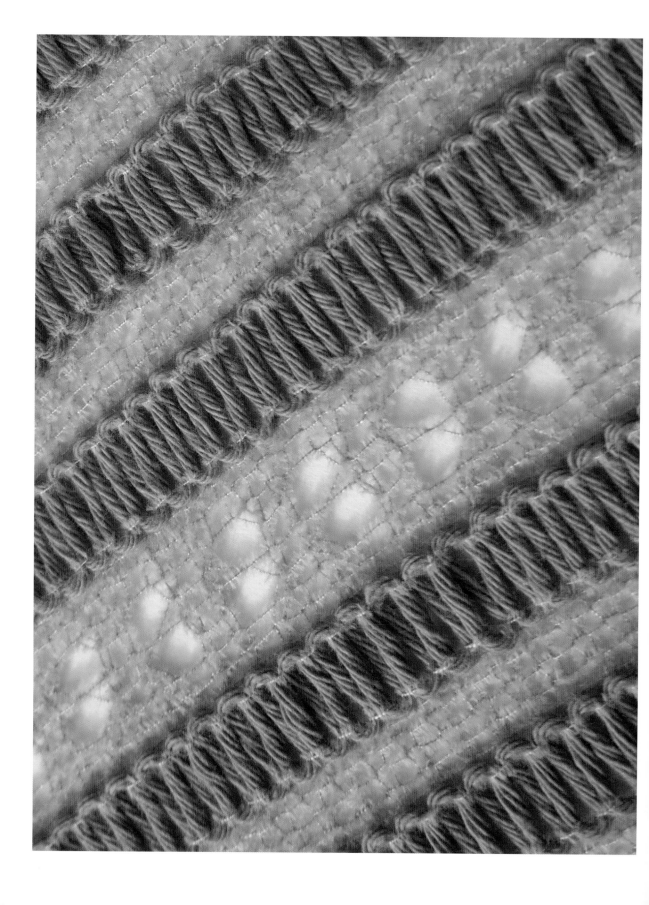

CONTENTS

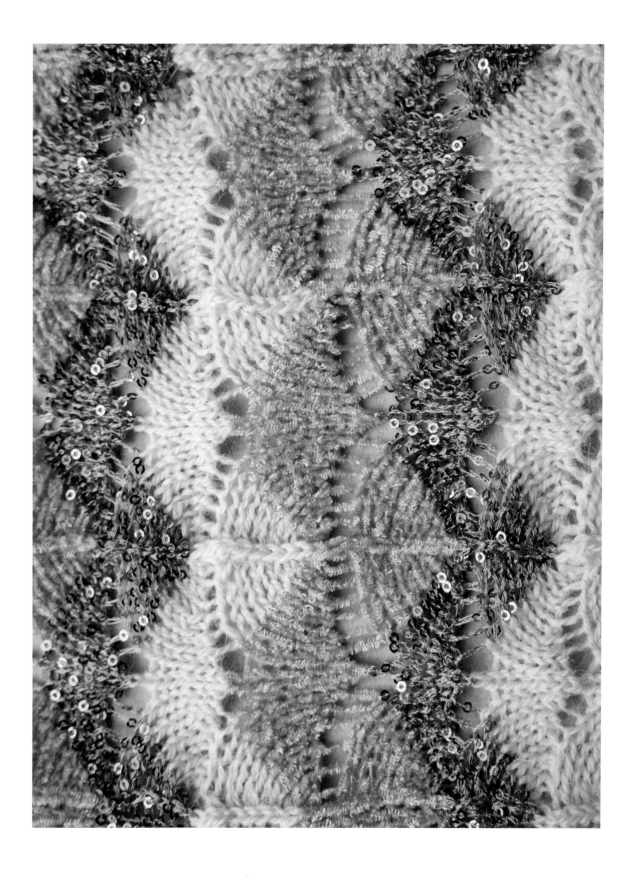

INTRODUCTION

have worked for a few years as a knitted swatch designer and that enabled me to spend a lot of time developing a variety of stitches. Lace has been one of my favourite techniques to experiment with as I particularly enjoy hand manipulating stitches. The fabrics produced by transferring stitches and creating open spaces have a special beauty to them and the creative possibilities are endless. In this book, I will share lace techniques I have learnt throughout the years, hoping to inspire you to practise and experiment with lace to develop some designs of your own.

The book begins by covering the basics, creating eyelets with simple and fully fashioned transfers, an introduction to charts and symbols, calculating the gauge and shaping knitted fabric. All techniques and stitches can be produced on most domestic knitting machines, except for those in Chapter 2 which focuses on the lace carriage for a Brother machine. This chapter takes you through the entire process of making a punch-card and tips for making a garment using the lace carriage.

Chapter 3 demonstrates that you do not always need to involve the knit carriage to create open fabrics. In this chapter you will learn how to knit and manipulate long stitches to create special fabrics, tuck stitches and adding beads to your knitting. If you have a double-bed knitting machine, Chapter 4 will cover the basics of casting on different types of ribbing. It moves on to some creative ideas to make your trims stand out by incorporating transfers to create a scalloped edge, combining lace techniques learnt in previous chapters with transfers between beds, and creating charts for double beds.

The yarn used for lace fabrics has a great impact on the outcome, therefore Chapter 5 will take techniques demonstrated in the book and show how you can experiment with yarn. I hope this chapter will encourage you to experiment and use yarns that you previously thought might be unsuitable for lace. In the last chapter, you will see the process of completing 4 projects of different complexity. I hope that seeing how a knitted accessory or garment is made from start to finish will give you confidence to make one for yourself or a loved one.

I am glad to be able to share all these techniques with you and I hope that you will find this book useful and inspirational.

Thank you.

Elena Berenghean

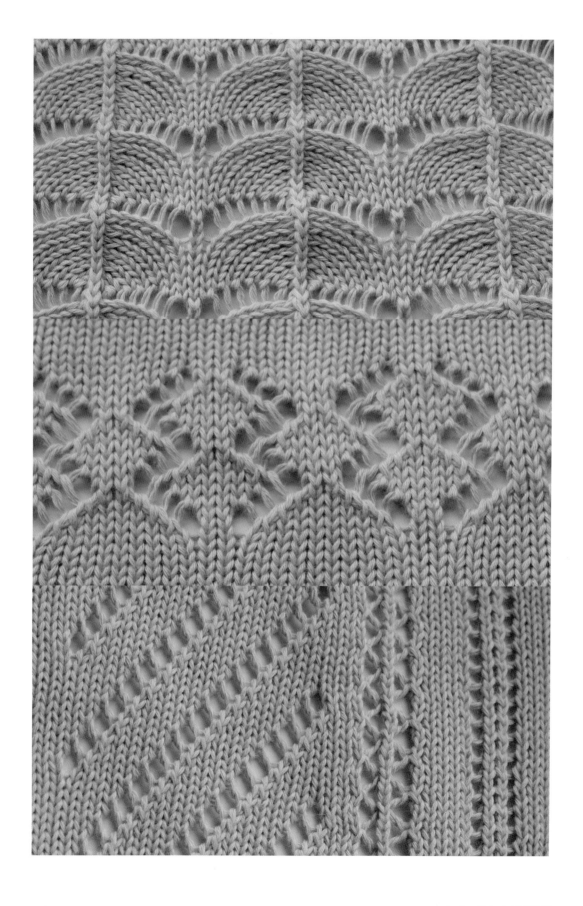

CHAPTER 1

EYELETS

n this chapter you will learn how to create eyelets by doing simple and fully fashioned transfers, understand what symbols are used when designing eyelets and how to use these symbols to plan a lace pattern on squared paper. This chapter also covers an introduction to calculating the gauge, shaping a knitted sample and blocking.

CREATING BASIC EYELETS

Eyelets are created by transferring one or multiple stitches at the same time and emptying a needle.

If the emptied needle is left in working position on the next knitting row, an eyelet is formed. A knitting machine usually comes with a set of standard transfer tools with 1, 2 or 3 prongs in different combinations. These tools are essential for creating eyelets amongst other techniques. If you would like to start practising eyelets but you are not sure how to cast on, check the 'Begin knitting lace' section in Chapter 2 where you can learn step-by-step how to do an e-wrap cast-on.

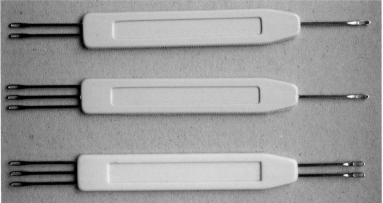

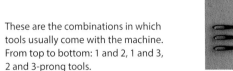
These are the combinations in which tools usually come with the machine. From top to bottom: 1 and 2, 1 and 3, 2 and 3-prong tools.

1. Pick a stitch to transfer, place your 1-prong tool on the hook of that needle and pull it all the way out.

2. Push the needle back so that the stitch slips off the needle and onto the transfer tool.

3. Going over the peg, transfer the stitch on the adjacent needle, in this case to the right.

4. Make sure to place that needle back in working position and knit 2 rows.

5. In the next knitting row, the needle will cast back on, and the eyelet will be formed.

6. The most common number of rows in between transfers is 2, but you could knit a different number if you prefer.

When the needle is left in non-working position, a ladder will be formed. If you have a single-bed knitting machine, ladders can be used in combination with lace patterns as borders to the design, just like you could add a purl stitch as a border if you had a ribber bed. There are other ways you can use a ladder stitch; it can be part of a design, combined with other techniques, or on its own. I strongly encourage you to have a go at it and develop some patterns using ladders as you could create some beautiful open fabrics.

The difference between eyelets and ladders

When creating ladders, you can choose to place the needle back in work at any time you want; when and how you do that can become a design feature or a design itself. As soon as you place the needle you emptied back in working position, it will cast on a stitch again and stop the ladder from forming.

A needle in working position has its hook almost in line with the gate pegs. This is also referred to as 'B' position, as the needle butt is aligned with the letter 'B' engraved on the machine. In this image, only one needle is in working position while the rest are in non-working position, pushed as far back as possible (with the butts aligned with 'A').

A ladder is essentially a float formed in between 2 needles in action. Ladders can be as wide as you like, which will depend on how many needles are left out of action in between.

To stop the ladder from forming you can either just push the needle back into working position or take the purl bar from the adjacent stitch, just as shown in this image, using a 1-prong tool.

Showing the difference between simply placing a needle back in work (left-hand side) and using the purl bar (right-hand side).

Weights

The number of weights needed when knitting a sample will depend on the number of needles in work, type of yarn and tension used and that applies when knitting lace as well. When knitting lace for the first time, if you feel too much resistance when transferring, it might mean that you are using too much weight. When working with transfers there is always a chance that you might drop a stitch; if you are using too much weight, the stitch will run and form an unwanted ladder that might be more difficult to fix. On the other hand, not having enough weight can also be an issue as stitches might drop or the fabric could pull as you transfer.

I have 50 needles in work while using 2 claw weights which I initially placed on my cast-on comb; as I knitted rows and the swatch grew, I kept on moving the weights upwards. From now on, I will keep moving them up at intervals of about 20 rows; the more needles in work the more weights are needed, and you might need to also place them at the centre of the fabric.

When hooking the claw weights, you must not worry about damaging the fabric; if you place and remove them gently the stitches will not be affected. If you are using the ribber weights when knitting on a single bed, make sure to use weight hangers and not to hook the weight directly onto the fabric as that could damage it. There are a broad range of weighting tools, and, with time and more practice, you will learn how to use them and to feel when the weight is just right.

Charting basic eyelets

Being able to read and create a chart, not exclusively for lace patterns, is an invaluable skill for a machine knitter; it enables you to be more creative and plan complex designs on squared paper. To begin designing and developing lace patterns you will need a squared paper notebook, a pencil or coloured pencils and a rubber.

Transfer using a 1-prong tool to the left. On row 2, the third stitch is transferred using a 1-prong tool on top of the second stitch.

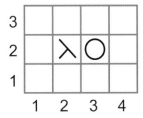

Transfer using a 1-prong tool to the right. On row 2, the second stitch is transferred using a 1-prong tool on top of the third stitch.

A pair of eyelets created using a 1-prong tool. On row 2, the second and fourth stitch are transferred on top of the third stitch. Needles 2 and 4 remain without a stitch and needle 3 has 3 stitches.

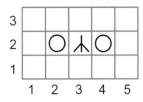

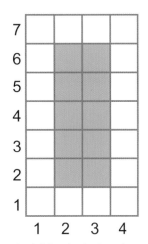
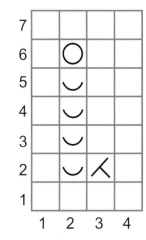

The left-hand side chart shows a 2-needle ladder beginning on row 2 and ending on row 6. The right-hand side chart shows that on row 2, the second stitch has been transferred to the right and its needle has been left in a non-working position until row 6, creating a 1-needle ladder.

Reading a chart is quite straightforward: every square represents a stitch horizontally and a row vertically. A chart is read from bottom to top, just as fabric grows on the machine. When you look at it, you must imagine you are looking at the fabric as it hangs off the machine, with the purl side facing you. The numbers on the left side of the chart represent rows and the numbers below represent stitches. If there is a symbol on row 2, for example, that means you need to do that action and then knit row 2.

Two of the symbols used when creating eyelets with a 1-prong tool are a circle that shows which needle is being emptied or where the lace hole will be created, and the tilted capital letter 'T' that shows on which needle the stitch is being transferred or the direction of the transfer. The direction of the transfer can sometimes be a design feature or make a sample look neater. When creating a pair of eyelets and 2 stitches are transferred on the same needle,

we have the 3-lines symbol that represents 3 stitches onto one needle.

There are 2 options available to chart or draw a ladder in a design or plan different patterns with ladders; you can use a semicircle symbol, or fill in the squares that represent needles out of action in a different colour. Make sure to write somewhere on your chart what every symbol or colour used means, to avoid confusion.

Next, you will see a collection of lace samples with the charts for each of these as examples of the variety of designs you can create. There are a few options I explored to make simple transfers a bit more interesting: combining transfers to the left and to the right and multiple repeat patterns in one sample, creating specific shapes, and mixing stockinette-stitch rows and lace repeats of different sizes. In a couple of these samples, you will notice that I combined transfers every 1 row and 2 rows. Spend time practising some of these samples and get comfortable with reading a chart before developing your own designs.

Samples and corresponding charts

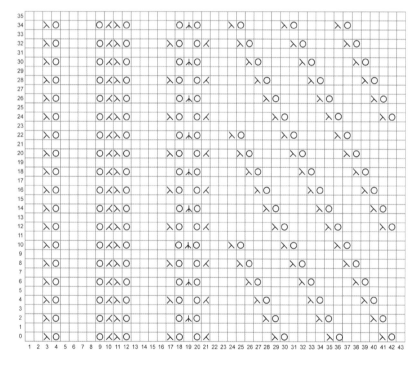
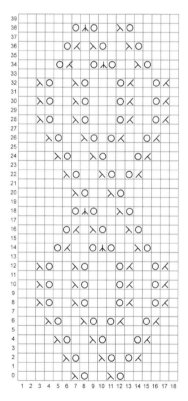

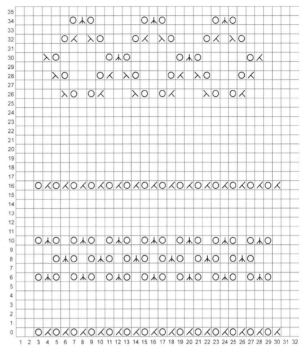

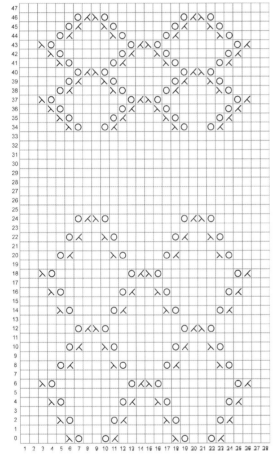

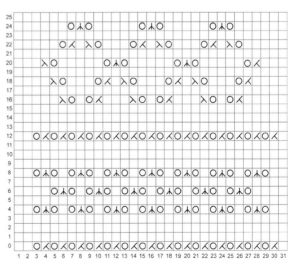

FULLY FASHIONED TRANSFERS

To produce a lace fabric with more depth you can use a multiple-stitch tool to transfer when creating eyelets; this is also referred to as a fully fashioned transfer. In a fully fashioned transfer, the empty needle and the one with 2 stitches are not next to each other. Depending on the tool you are using there might be 2, 3 or more stitches in between.

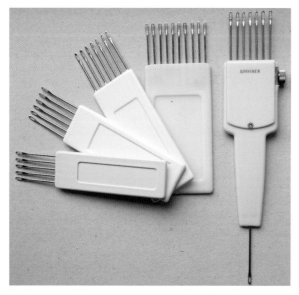

Tools come in different sizes and can also be adjustable; they will make multiple stitch transfers much easier. These tools don't usually come with the machine but can easily be purchased online.

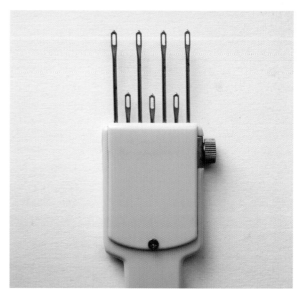

By loosening and tightening the side screw you can create your unique combination tool. With this tool you could transfer every other needle and create 4 eyelets at once, which will make the process much faster.

STEP-BY-STEP: FORMING AN EYELET BY TRANSFERRING USING A 3-PRONG TOOL

1. Hold your finger against the fabric and, using a 3-prong tool, pick up 3 stitches and pull the needles all the way out.

2. Push the needles back so that the 3 stitches are sliding off the needles and onto the transfer tool.

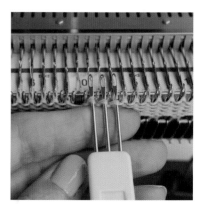

3. Going over the pegs, transfer the 3 stitches all together to the right to empty one needle.

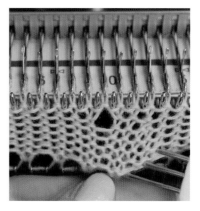

4. Lifting the tool like so as you complete the transfer can help you avoid dropping stitches.

5. Make sure to place the needle you emptied back in working position and knit 2 rows.

6. After knitting the 2 rows, the needle will cast on and an eyelet will be formed.

The more stitches you are transferring at once the greater the risk of dropping them. In this example I am transferring using a 7-prong tool. I have pulled the needles out and pushed them back; all 7 stitches are on the tool.

Before transferring the stitches to the right, I will use the tool to pull the needles back in working position, so they are ready to receive the stitches. This will make life a little bit easier and the process faster.

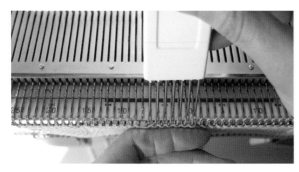

If you do not have these tools, you can do the transfer in 2 or 3 steps using the standard ones. To transfer 7 stitches, you can transfer 3 then 2 stitches twice or hold the tools together.

Charting fully fashioned transfers

Just like in a chart with basic eyelets, the circle and tilted capital letter 'T' symbols are used when charting fully fashioned transfers. The slanting-stitch symbol will help you differentiate between them, and depending on the direction of the transfer, it is drawn either as a line tilted to the left or to the right. The slanting stitches are what will give the decorative effect to your sample as their orientation will change once they are transferred. The more stitches you transfer at once, the more dramatic the effect.

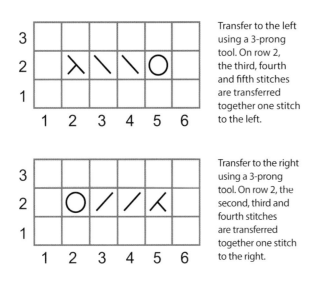

Transfer to the left using a 3-prong tool. On row 2, the third, fourth and fifth stitches are transferred together one stitch to the left.

Transfer to the right using a 3-prong tool. On row 2, the second, third and fourth stitches are transferred together one stitch to the right.

A pair of eyelets created using a 3-prong tool. On row 2, the second, third and fourth stitches are transferred one stitch to the right. The sixth, seventh and eighth stitches are transferred one stitch to the left.

You can also combine the number of stitches transferred to produce an eyelet within a pattern; the most common is either increasing or decreasing the number of stitches transferred. For example, a repeat begins by transferring one stitch, and every 2 rows the number of stitches transferred is increased by one with every new transfer. For these types of transfers, having multiple stitch tools will save you a lot of time and trouble.

☐ - purl ▨ - ladder (needle out of work) - lace repeat - 10 rows & 22 stitches

⅄\\O - transfer using a three prong tool to the left O//⅄ - transfer using a three prong tool to the right

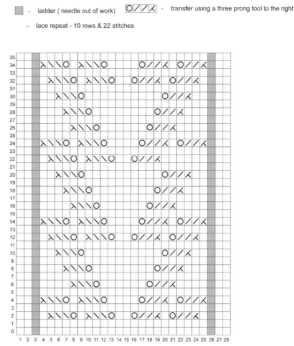

This chart shows how you can write what all the symbols represent or other information about the sample.

Example of a repeat of fully fashioned transfers

In this sample you can observe the use of a ladder as a border to the lace pattern.

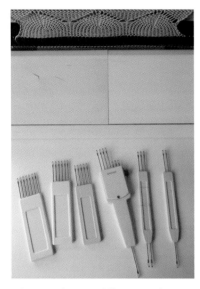

When transferring a different number of stitches every one or two rows, I like to have tools for each of these transfers prepared on my lap. I also keep them in the order I will be using them.

Examples of combined fully fashioned transfers

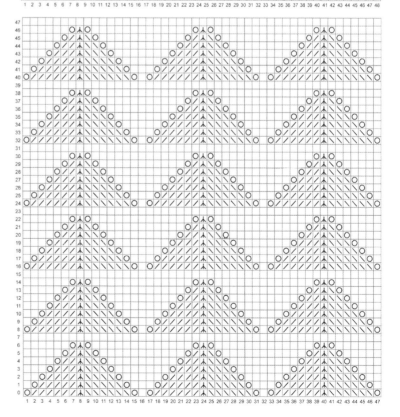

Blocking knitted lace samples

Blocking is the last step in completing a project; it will even out the stitches, give the fabric more drape and make your finished project look polished and professional. You can even fix any minor sizing issues in a knitted piece by blocking it to the correct size.

Blocking is particularly important for lace fabrics as it will help stretch and reveal all the details in your patterns. It really depends on the fibre, stitch and tension used; every lace fabric is different. There are 2 main methods of blocking, steam blocking and wet blocking. In time, with experience, you will learn how different fabrics behave and what method of blocking works better but when in doubt, use the wet blocking method.

Pins, measuring tape and a soft surface are needed to block knitted fabrics. You can purchase special blocking mats for knitwear with grids printed on them which will help you align the edges of your samples. I am using kids' gym mats, an inexpensive alternative which has worked well for me so far. However, I am considering investing in some knitwear blocking mats in the future.

STEP-BY-STEP: WET BLOCKING A SAMPLE

1. This is how a sample looks as I have taken it off the machine; it is a little wrinkled, the edges are curling, and the lace pattern is not perfectly visible.

2. Fill a basin with luke-warm water and add a little delicate or wool detergent. Do not agitate or shake the fabric too much, you can just leave it for a few minutes until the fabric is properly soaked.

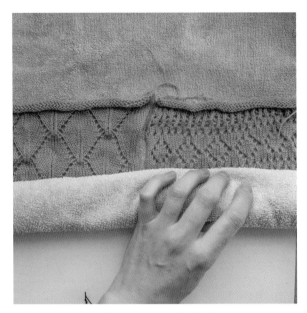

3. Drain the water and gently squeeze the fabric to remove as much liquid as possible without wringing it. Rolling your samples in a towel is a great way to remove the excess water.

4. Pin the fabric without stretching it too much, ideally to the size you want to achieve and let it dry. Some fabrics might not need to be pinned as they will sit flat on their own.

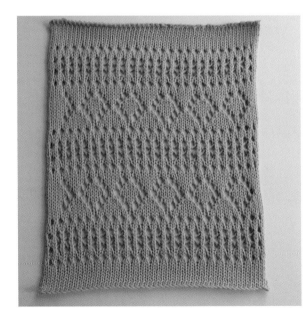

5. Once dried, the sample should hold its shape when you unpin it, but it really depends on the fibre you are using; natural fibres tend to hold their shape better.

Tension

The stitch size is determined by the tension setting on the carriage tension dial. When the tension dial is set to 0 it will create the smallest stitch size (tightest tension). When the tension dial is set to 10 it will create the largest stitch size (loosest tension). The dial is graduated from 0 to 10; in between the numbers there are 2 dots. If the dial points to the first dot after number 5, for instance, that means the tension used is 5.1.

You must adjust the dial by rotating it according to the yarn you are using. The thicker the yarn, the looser the tension.

Gauge

If you want to knit a piece of fabric of a desired size or make a garment, you will have to calculate the gauge. Gauge simply refers to the number of stitches and rows of a specific size of a swatch; most commonly 10cm. Even if 2 samples are knitted on the same machine, the yarn and tension used will influence the stitch size and thus the gauge.

When it comes to lace, it is often not as straightforward as that. Besides the factors mentioned above, stitch will also determine the gauge; and that applies to other techniques such as cables, tucks and so forth. Even when using the same yarn and tension, a sample knitted in stockinette stitch and a sample with multiple

stitch transfers might come out in different sizes. Also, it can be difficult to count stitches once they have been transferred and their orientation is changed.

For example, if a sample that is 40 stitches by 40 rows measures 13cm, that means there are 40 stitches in 13cm. If we divide the number of stitches by its width, we can learn how many stitches we have per 1cm: $40 \div 13 = 3.07$; that means that there are approximately 3 stitches per 1cm. To put this into practice, if we want to knit a sample that is 30cm wide, we must calculate: $3.07 \times 30 = 92.1$. Therefore, to knit this sample we must cast on 92 stitches (I usually round numbers up to have an even number of stitches).

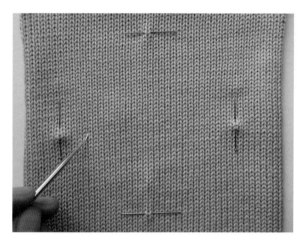

To calculate the gauge, mark a 10cm area on your sample with pins and count the number of stitches and rows. Once you have learnt your gauge, you will be able to use it to knit a sample with specific measurements. It is very important to mention that the gauge is calculated after the sample has been steamed and/or washed, as some fibres such as wool will shrink.

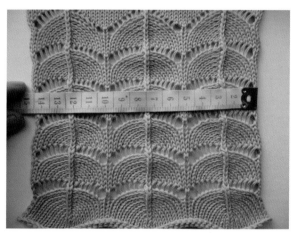

To calculate the gauge of a lace knitted fabric I usually work backwards by first knitting a sample and noting the specific number of stitches and rows then measuring it.

Calculations

You don't need to be a maths wizard to be able to calculate increases or decreases to create a knitted piece in the desired shape and size. However, if you are one, you can create formulas to help with your process; below, you will see the basic calculation you need to do to evenly increase or decrease. The gauge will help you convert cm to stitches and rows.

To use as an example, let's say that we must decrease from 86 to 74 stitches (12 stitches in total) in 90 rows. To learn the number of rows we must knit in between every decrease. We must first divide the number of rows by the number of decreases:

$90 \div 2 = 7.5$

This tells us there will be a decrease of one stitch every 7.5 rows. It is not possible to decrease every 7.5 rows, therefore it must be a combination of decreases every 7 and 8 rows. We could try to figure out how many times we need to decrease every 7 and every 8 rows, and space them evenly.

But for simplicity we can do a work around. We can multiply the number of stitches to be decreased with the number of rows: $7 \times 12 = 84$

This means that if we decrease 12 times every 7 rows, we would knit 84 rows, which is very close to 90. To make our lives easier we can just add the extra 6 rows either before the first, or after the last decrease and continue decreasing every 7 rows for the rest of the sample.

Shaping knitted fabric

The best part about knitwear is that it can be zero-waste; that means you can increase and decrease stitches to give a swatch an exact shape. By increasing and decreasing you can create necklines or armholes, and produce a garment to the fit you want. In some special instances you might have to cut and sew to make a garment but with the example shown previously, you should be able to plan increases and decreases to avoid that. I am a big fan of fully fashioned knitwear, it has a special beauty to it. I will also show you some ideas to make your fashioning even more beautiful.

Decreasing

Step 1: Use a 2-prong tool to pick up the last 2 stitches on the left side and transfer them onto the adjacent needle. You can choose to transfer a different number of stitches.

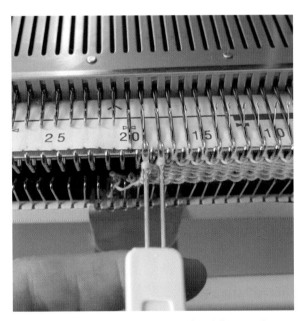

Step 2: The sample has now one less stitch and the second needle has 2 stitches. I am decreasing on the left side of my swatch, which will shape the right edge on the knit side of the fabric.

Increasing

Step 1: Place a new needle in work and using a 2-prong tool, transfer both stitches at the edge, one stitch to the left. You have emptied one needle and the swatch has one extra stitch.

Step 2: To avoid producing an eyelet, take the purl bar from the needle on the left or right and place it on the empty needle.

Decreasing and increasing when knitting lace fabric is not very different or more difficult. When decreasing using a 3-prong tool, for example, there will be 4 stitches involved in that transfer; 3 being transferred, one receiving a new stitch. Make sure to not create any lace holes using those 4 stitches so you can achieve a neat edge. You can also plan decreases on squared paper to know exactly where to stop the pattern. However, if you choose not to plan decreases on squared paper, make sure you first decrease, then transfer to create eyelets. Note: Always test a decrease before starting the final project.

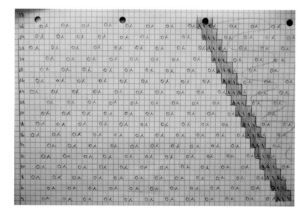

In this chart I mapped the decreases using a second colour. I will be decreasing using a 3-prong tool; this will show me where I can form the last eyelet on every row.

This created a little border and would also give the seam more structure. If you do not want to create this border you can transfer using a 1-prong tool when decreasing.

Details when shaping knitted fabric

If you want to take the fashioning of a garment to the next level, you can add little stitch details when decreasing or increasing.

An easy way to incorporate lace holes in your fashioning is to do it the 'lazy way' by simply transferring the stitches to increase without taking the purl bar to form a new stitch before knitting any rows. I usually do this when I shape the sleeves of a jumper.

Including ladders can be another way to add details to the shaping and there are so many ways to do that. For this swatch, I first transferred to empty 2 needles to form a ladder, then transferred all the stitches to the left and 3 on the right of the ladder to decrease.

KNITTING TIPS

- When knitting your samples, make sure to leave at least 2 stitches at the edges without any lace holes. This way the edge will be neat, and it will be easier to sew the sides when making garments.
- When creating pairs of eyelets, pull the needle with 3 stitches all the way out before knitting any rows, as there is a risk of the needle not completing the stitch properly. If the carriage is in holding position, pull the needle out but make sure to push it back about halfway so it can be selected by the carriage when you knit across.
- Make sure to write as much information or as many instructions as you can on your chart; I usually do that at the top of the page to make reading the chart as clear as possible.

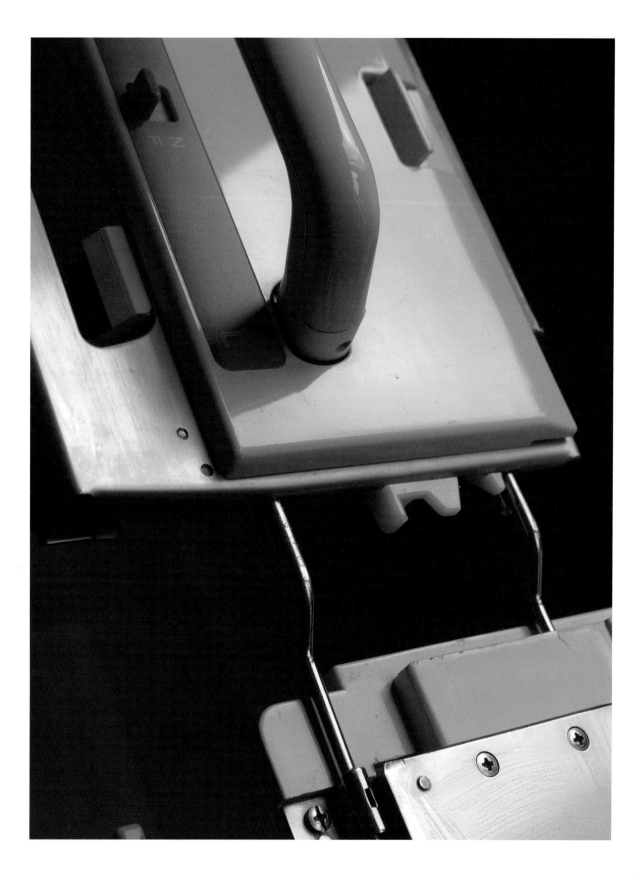

CHAPTER 2

LACE CARRIAGE

n this chapter, I will introduce a faster way to knit simple lace patterns: the lace carriage. Many knitting machine models come with a lace carriage and all the information on how to use them will be found in the user manual. Some models such as Knitmaster, also known as a Silver Reed, and some Toyota models will have carriages that transfer stitches and knit. In this chapter I will demonstrate how to use the lace carriage on a Brother knitting machine, which only transfers stitches.

The lace carriage – Brother knitting machines

The Brother lace carriage is used together with the knit carriage and they both remain on the machine. Using the extension rails, you will be able to do alternating courses without the risk of carriages crashing into each other or falling off the machine. The lace carriage rolls the punch-card, selects needles as per the punch-card and transfers the stitches. The main carriage is set to 'NL' and knits across after the lace carriage transfers.

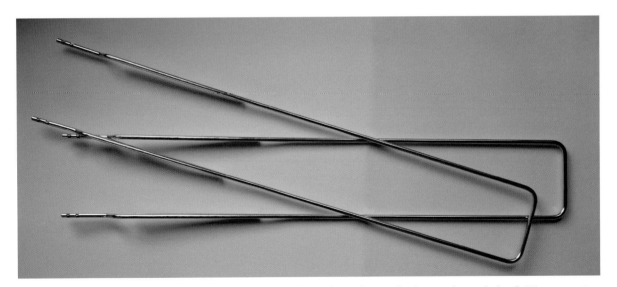

The extension rails will enable you to take the carriages off and back on the machine easily; they are also used when knitting garments and having all the needles in work.

The lace carriage has 2 settings; 'N' (normal) and 'F' (fine). When the carriage is set to 'N', the transfers are done in the same way as transferring to the left using a 1-prong tool. When the carriage is set to 'F', the stitch is split between the needle selected and the one to the left and no needle is left empty.

The lace carriage can be set to knit fine lace ('F'), which only part-transfers the stitch or normal lace ('N'), which creates an eyelet in the same way as when doing manual transfers. When knitting simple lace using the carriage, the stitches are transferred to the left and the last needle on both sides will not transfer so that the edges are neat. You can combine normal and fine lace when knitting one single sample; experiment and see what looks best depending on the lace design. I like to combine sections of fine and normal lace as different textured stripes.

Punch-cards for simple lace

A punch-card is used when creating lace with the carriage in a similar way to when knitting 2-colour Fair Isle patterns, for example. On a Brother machine, when you insert the punch-card in the card reader, the machine will read 7 rows below the row in view.

You can purchase pre-punched lace cards, the Brother has a wide variety of lace patterns which can be found online, or you can design your own.

Using squared paper is probably the easiest way to develop patterns and create your own lace punch-cards. When developing repeats, you must take into consideration that the card is 24 stitches.

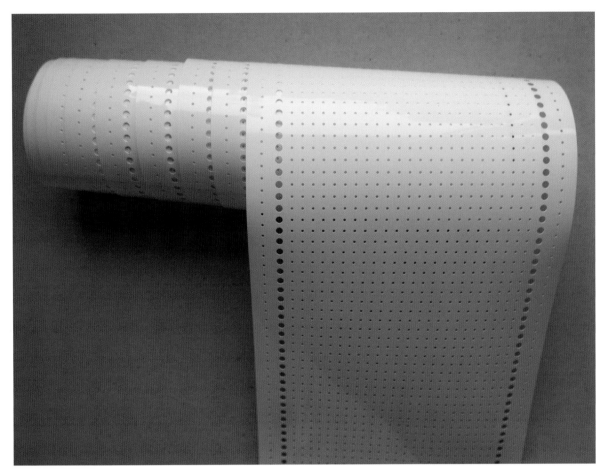

Punch-cards can be purchased as a blank roll of different lengths and can be cut according to the number of rows of your lace repeat.

The 24-stitch design will repeat across your knitted sample; if you have 48 needles in work, the design will repeat twice and so forth. Your designs do not necessarily have to be a repeat pattern – abstract shapes can also look pretty.

When starting to develop designs, keep in mind that when you punch the card, you must leave at least one square or stitch in between every hole punched so that the stitch has an adjacent needle to be transferred onto. If 2 holes are punched next to each other there is a high chance of stitches dropping and causing irregularities in your swatch. That is also something to keep in mind when you are knitting: if your machine keeps on dropping stitches

for no apparent reason, double check the punch-card and ensure you have not punched 2 holes next to each other. Every punched hole on the card will be a needle selected by the lace carriage and an eyelet on your fabric. If you did find a mistake in your punch-card, you can use tape to cover the hole which was punched in the wrong place; I like to use Scotch Magic Tape and cut a piece small enough to cover the specific hole on both sides of the punch-card.

Lace punch-cards for Brother, or other models that have lace carriages which only transfer, are characterised by intervals of blank or unpunched rows. For simple lace, when punching the card, in between every punched row leave a blank one. That row accounts for one of the courses that the lace carriage does: one course to select the needles and one to do the transfers. The lace carriage rolls the card on every course; that blank row will ensure that no needles are selected before knitting rows with the main carriage. When designing on squared paper, you can draw your design without having these rows in between if that is easier and only add them when transferring the pattern on the card.

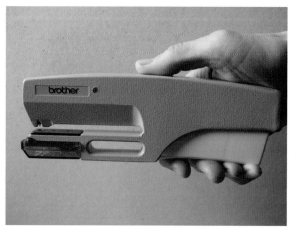

You will need a card punch to create holes in the punch-card; the model I am using is KA-541 and I purchased it together with my knitting machine.

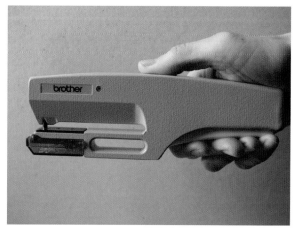

It is very easy to use; to punch a hole, squeeze the punch grip until the cutter removes the square selected.

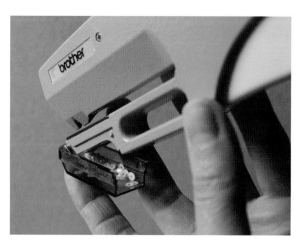

The cuttings will accumulate in the plastic reservoir, which can be emptied by pressing downwards on the lid lip of the case.

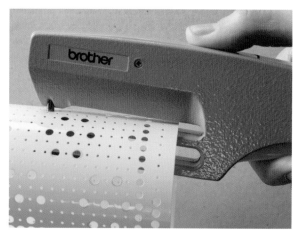

The card punch can fit in its jaw half of the punch-card width; you will have to punch one side at a time.

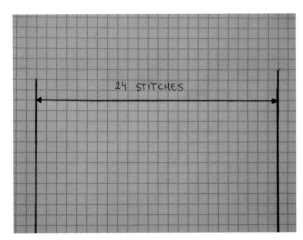

1. Draw 2 parallel lines to mark the 24 stitches area on the squared paper, you can always tape more pages if you need more rows for your repeat.

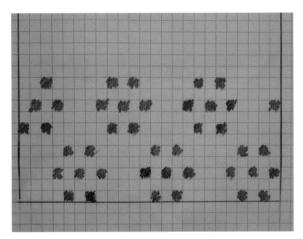

2. Begin mapping the design by filling in squares with a pencil; all the squares marked are where you will punch the card and the eyelets will be created.

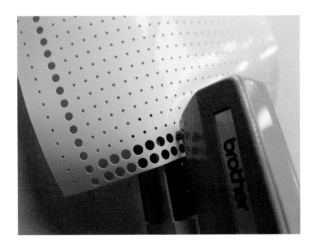

3. Punch 2 rows of holes at the very bottom; the card ends will overlap, and the 2 rows punched at the bottom (and at the top) will allow that.

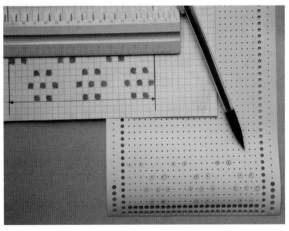

4. Transfer the design on the punch-card. I like to use a needle pusher to reveal one row at a time – and so I don't make mistakes.

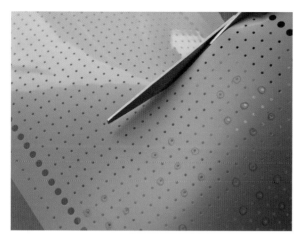

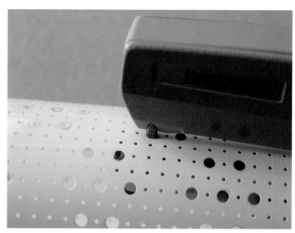

5. When finishing drawing the pattern on the punch-card, you can cut the card from the roll. Make sure to include the 2 extra rows of holes.

6. Select a square, guide the card in the jaws of the punch until the guide pin locates the pin hole in the square and squeeze the punch to create the hole.

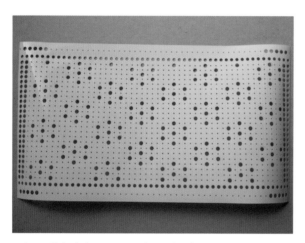

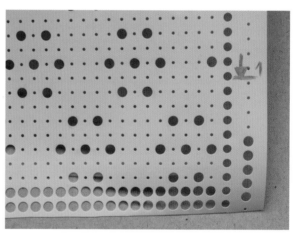

7. Once all the holes are created, punch a few on the edges of both ends. These are connecting holes and the plastic snaps will be placed in them.

8. Mark row 1, 7 rows above the first row of the pattern. This will be the row in view when the card reader reads the first row of the repeat.

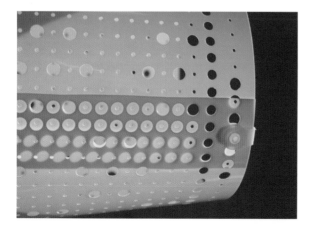

9. When the card is in the reader, this is how its ends are overlapped and clipped together with the plastic snaps to knit the pattern repeatedly.

RIGHT: You might find it easier to develop patterns by first drawing shapes and lines to guide you. Have a go at it and see what kind of shapes you can create; the process of developing patterns is a fun one.

BELOW: This is an example of how you can fill in squares where you want the eyelets to be; the lace holes could also be on the outside of the shapes I have drawn. There are no limitations if you leave at least one stitch in between.

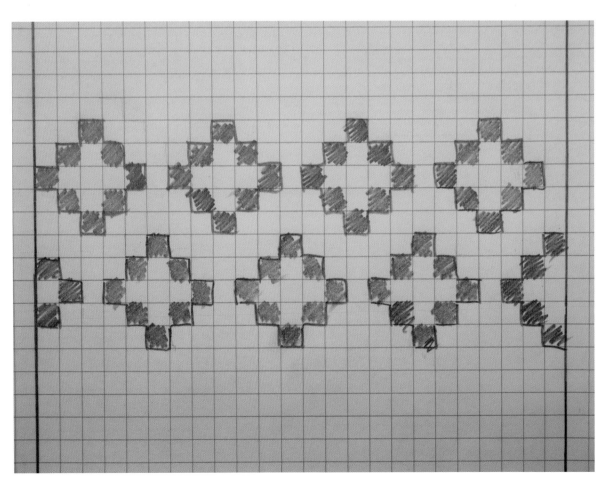

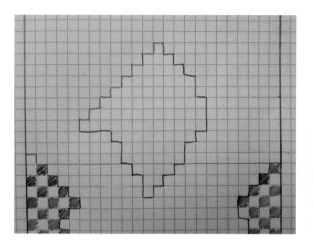

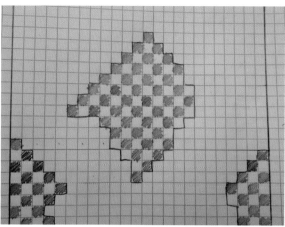

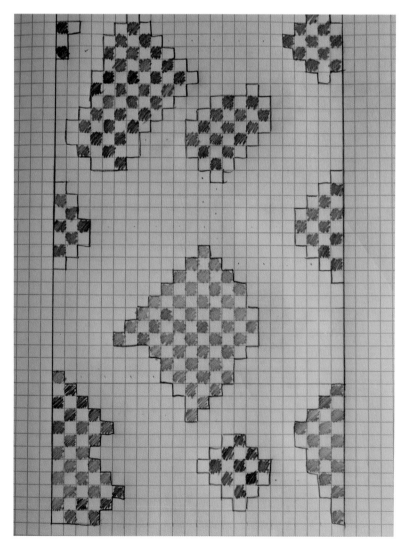

ABOVE LEFT: If you would like to create an abstract design, you can draw abstract shapes in the same way as the previous example. These types of patterns can look attractive when using the fine setting on the carriage ('F').

ABOVE RIGHT: In this example I am filling every other square inside the shape I have drawn. I am making sure that when the design repeats across, there will not be 2 filled-in squares next to each other.

LEFT: The whole design on squared paper. This is just an initial development; at this point I don't know how it will turn out, but I don't worry too much about whether it will be successful – the first sample is rarely perfect.

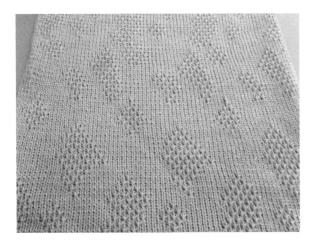

The sample knitted using the 'F' (fine) setting on the lace carriage.

A sample knitted using the same punch-card in normal ('N') lace.

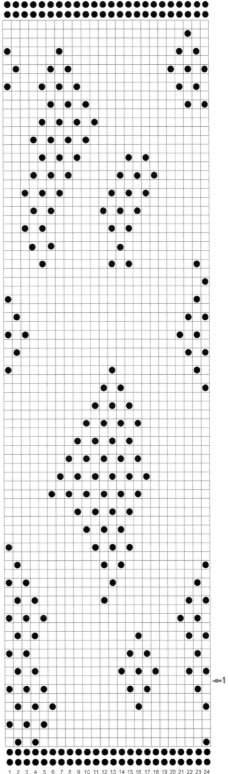

Chart including the blank rows. The punch-card will come out quite long due to the blank rows in between.

Two more lace patterns for the lace carriage with charts

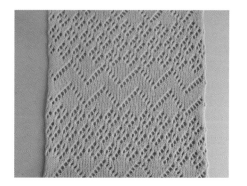

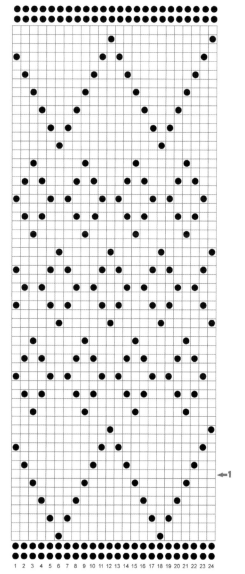

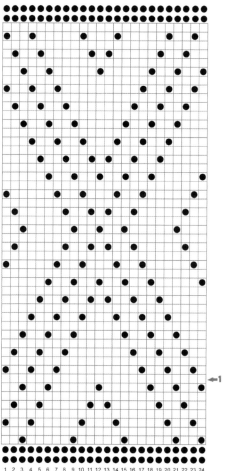

Begin knitting lace

To begin, cast on a sample and knit a few rows with the main carriage. Make sure that the knit carriage ends up on the right after knitting these rows. The rule is that you begin with the knit carriage on the right, and the lace carriage on the left where they must return every single time. You can knit as many rows as you want with the knit carriage, but it must be more than one. When doing simple transfers, the lace carriage does 2 courses, one to select needles and one to transfer stitches. You can keep track of the row number for your sample, as the row counter will only be tripped by the knit carriage.

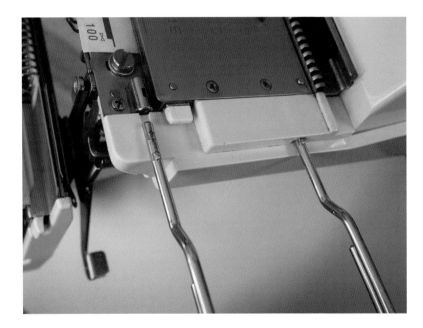

Insert the extension rails in the 2 holes on both side of the machine. You know they are placed properly when they click in and stay secure.

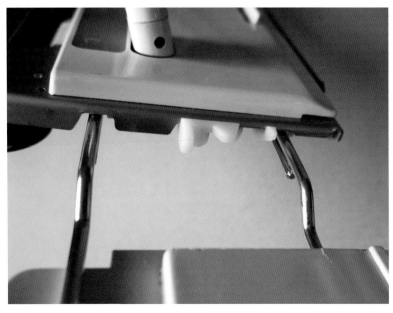

Slide the lace carriage on the extension rail; do a quick check back and forth to test. If the punch-card belt starts moving, the carriage is placed correctly.

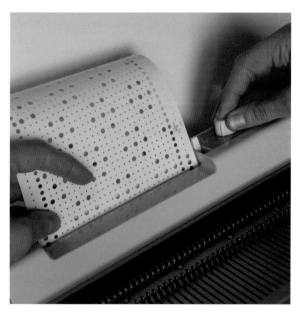

1. Keeping the punch-card straight, insert it in the card reader and feed it by pressing and rotating the dial to the left. Clip the card to form a continuous loop.

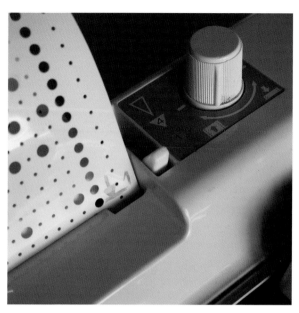

2. Lock the punch-card on the row marked '1' by moving the lever to the circle symbol. The card must be locked for the first pass of the lace carriage.

3. Move the lace carriage across from left to right; needles are selected and brought forward as per the first row of your punch-card.

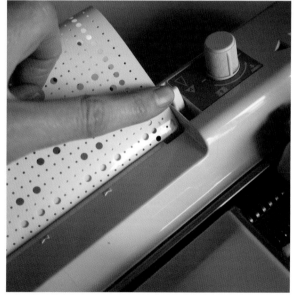

4. Unlock the card by moving the lever to the triangle symbol in the middle. From now on the punch-card will roll with every pass of the lace carriage.

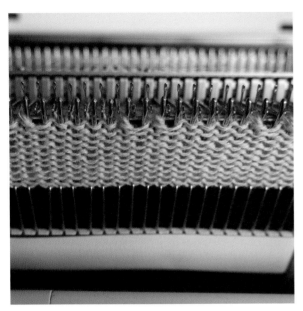

5. Move the lace carriage from right to left to do the transfers. All needles that were brought forward in the previous row will be without the stitch.

6. Knit across with the main carriage (from right to left). In this example I have knitted 2 rows, and the main carriage returned on the right.

7. Repeat that 3 times to complete half of the repeat; once half of the repeat is complete, knit 6 rows.

Knitting a different number of rows between specific sections of a lace pattern can be a way to do more variations of a design. This can simply be a way to create a less open fabric or make sections of a pattern more obvious. You may also use the lace carriage to easily introduce small lace sections in combination with other hand-manipulated stitches.

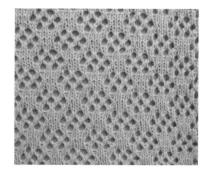
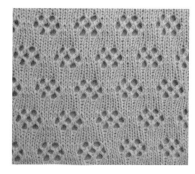

The same lace pattern with 2 rows in between every transfer (left-hand side) and one with sections of 6 rows in between repeats (right-hand side). The flower motif is hardly noticeable in the sample with 2 rows in between.

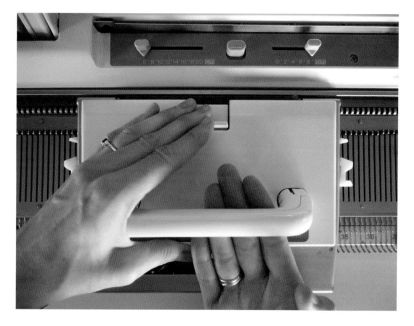

If the lace carriage gets jammed, to remove it press the release button towards you and lift the carriage. Take care when removing the carriage to not catch the needles as there is a risk of breaking or bending them. Once you remove the carriage, ensure that the needles are aligned and in correct working position and rotate the dial to return the punch-card to the appropriate place.

Quick waste yarn cast-on

A waste yarn cast-on can be useful when using the lace carriage if you wish to begin transferring and having lace holes right at the bottom of your sample. When casting on with the main yarn and passing the lace carriage after the first or second row there is a chance of the yarn snapping, especially when using a more fragile one. By beginning with waste yarn, and then e-wrapping the main yarn, you can start transferring even after the first row as there will be enough fabric to attach the weight on, and the

cast-on comb is out of the way. In some instances, doing a waste yarn cast-on can be a way to reduce unhappy accidents when knitting.

The method shown next can also be used as a 'quick cast-on' of the main yarn, when you want to test samples and do not want to spend too much time casting on. Even though it will produce a looser first row, which can be unaesthetic, it will not allow a sample to unravel. If you would like to use a normal cast-on by e-wrapping, begin with Step 3.

1. Using a needle pusher, bring every other needle into working position and knit one row in waste yarn. Hook the comb and attach the claw weights.

2. Put the rest of the needles in work and knit a few rows in waste yarn; about 10 or 15. After knitting the last row, make sure the carriage ends up on the right.

3. Take your main yarn, pull the needles all the way out. Create a slipknot, place it on the first needle on the left and secure it by gently pulling the tail.

4. To begin e-wrapping, bring the yarn up in between the second and third needle and go around the second needle like the lower-case letter 'e'.

5. Press your finger gently under the needle to hold the previous loop and continue e-wrapping; try to keep an even tension and not wrap too tightly.

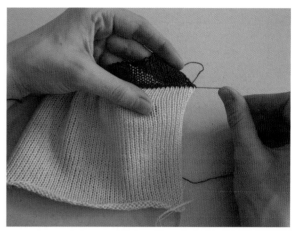

6. To remove the waste yarn, snap the last loop on the opposite side where the tail is and pull it to unravel the entire row. The sample should come off easily.

Lace carriage and making a garment

I made a vest top a while ago using the lace carriage for the front panel and when I got to the part where I had to shape the neckline, I realised that I could not knit short rows and use the lace carriage at the same time; the lace carriage was crashing into the needles that were in 'E', or holding position. Usually to shape a round neckline you must do it one side at a time: you place half the needles on hold, shape one side of the neckline, cast off and shape the other side. You might not feel ready to make an entire garment just yet, but when you are ready, do bear this in mind.

I did find a solution to shaping my neckline that enabled me to continue the lace pattern all the way to the top. This method can work for a V-neck jumper as well. Other knitting machine models might allow you to do short rows when using the lace carriage so you might be able to shape a neckline as any other time.

Introduction to short rows

When knitting a short row, it means that you are knitting only part of a row. To do that you must place some of the needles on that row in holding position. If, for example, your sample is 20 stitches and you place half of the needles in holding position, when knitting across, the row will become shorter. If you place more needles in holding position the row becomes even shorter, as you have less needles knitting. If you place needles back in work instead, the row becomes longer.

If the carriage is on the side where the needles are in holding position, a long float will be created over these needles which is not something that is usually desired. When needles are just placed in holding position without also setting the holding cam lever on the carriage to 'H', the needles will knit normally, and no stitches will be dropped.

ABOVE: A needle on hold is pulled all the way out so that its butt is aligned with letter 'E' engraved on the machine bed.

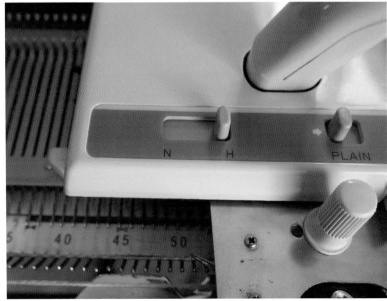

RIGHT: To set the carriage to hold for the Brother, put the holding cam lever from 'N' to 'H'; check the manual to learn how to put the carriage in holding position for the machine model you are using.

LEFT: This sample has 50 stitches. Half the needles are in working position, half in holding position. The carriage is on the side where needles remain in work.

BELOW: When knitting across, only the needles in working position will knit; all the needles that are pulled all the way out will not. I could now shape if this was one side of my neckline.

1. You have finished your body and you are ready to start shaping the neckline. Take a note of the row you are currently on and mark the punch-card – it can be as simple as a little line in pencil.

2. Cast off the centre of the neckline starting from right to left. This is just a test sample, so I cast off 20 stitches. Pick up the last stitch on the right side to avoid getting a little hole.

3. Place the carriage and all the needles on the left-hand side in holding position. Knit a few rows in a contrast colour waste yarn with the needles that remain in work.

4. Drop all the stitches in waste yarn and keep this side out of the way. The number of weights must be reduced as the number of needles in work has now more than halved.

5. Push the needles back and move the row counter back to the row you were on before knitting rows in waste yarn. You can now continue the lace pattern on this side and shape according to your calculations.

6. Once you have finished one half of the neckline, you can hook back up the other half, using a tool or manually pushing the needles through the loops. You can see why using a contrast colour waste yarn is helpful.

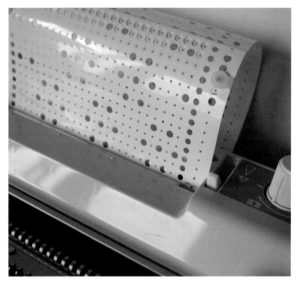

7. Pull the needles all the way out, if you haven't already when hooking the stitches back on the needles, and carefully unravel the waste yarn. To avoid dropping stitches, attach a couple of claw weights.

8. Set your row counter back to the number you had when you started shaping the other side, rotate the dial of the card reader to return the punch-card to the mark you have made and lock the card.

9. After doing the first course with the lace carriage you can unlock the card and continue knitting the lace pattern, decreasing the same way you did on the other side of the neckline.

I used a 1-prong tool to do the decreases when using the lace carriage. By transferring over only one stitch, the needle with 2 stitches will be right at the edge (or the last needle) and the lace carriage will not select it.

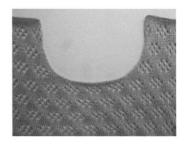

The sample after being washed and blocked. I can now add a rib trim or a crochet trim around the edge. Make sure to check your manual; other machine models might have the option to do short rows when creating lace.

TIPS FOR USING THE LACE CARRIAGE

- If your lace design is an all-over repeat, accommodate enough repeats so that when you cut the card it is at least 20cm long. If the card is too short, you might have difficulties inserting, overlapping, and clipping it in the card reader.
- Punch-cards can be purchased as a blank roll or with row numbers already written on the right side of the card; those will be useful to guide you on row 1. After that the row counter will not correspond to the rows on the card – I wouldn't recommend these cards as they are more useful for knitting Fair Isle, where the rows correspond to the knitting row.
- Write instructions on the card or on a separate page according to the outcome you would like to achieve. You can write marks or notes depending on how many rows you should knit in between transfers if you have more than 2 rows. Use letter 'N' or 'F' if you want to combine fine and normal lace on the same sample and so forth. Find your own way of writing instructions to make your life as easy as possible when knitting lace.

The difference between Brother and Silver Reed

As mentioned at the beginning of the chapter, some machine models will have lace carriages that operate differently to the Brother version. I have never used a Silver Reed machine, but I have watched a few instructional videos. My main take was that, when it comes to the lace carriage, it does seem that the Silver Reed is much easier to use. It has a separate carriage, just like the main carriage, that will do the transferring and the knitting as well. For this reason, there is no need for the extension rails on the Silver Reed.

The punch-cards are also different as there is no need for the blank rows; on the Silver Reed you can switch the lace carriage from the knitting setting and transferring setting. The carriage only rolls the card when it is set to do the transferring, and when you switch it to the knitting setting it will knit and trip the row counter. All these features are fantastic and extremely useful. If you do have a Silver Reed machine and would like to try the lace patterns shown in the previous pages, you can do so by transferring the patterns on your punch-card without the blank rows in between. Another important difference between the way these machines operate when using the punch-card is that Brother will read 7 rows below the row in view and Silver Reed will read 5 rows below.

If you own a knitting machine that is not a Brother or a Silver Reed, make sure to consult the user manual to learn what type of punch-card is compatible with your machine.

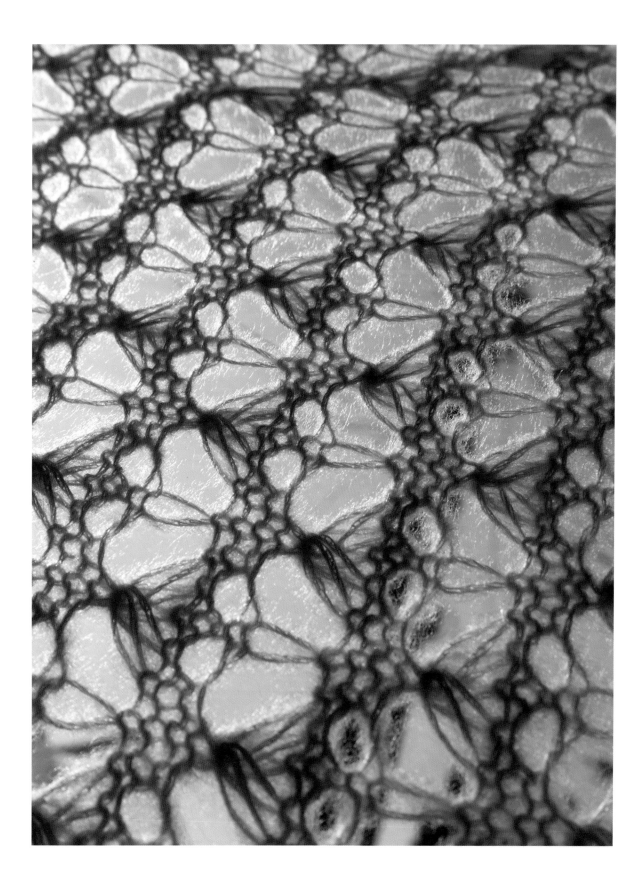

CHAPTER 3

LONG-STITCH OPEN FABRICS

This chapter looks at different ways of creating open fabrics and some techniques that can be produced without using the carriage. You will learn how to create long stitches, how to manipulate these stitches to achieve a different effect and how to add beads into your knitting.

SIMPLE LONG STITCHES

Long stitches are essentially normal knit or purl stitches but elongated. When stitches are elongated, the fabric automatically has an openness to it. These are beautiful but quite time-consuming techniques, as they involve more manual labour than regular machine knitting. If you would like to incorporate long-stitch rows in your garment but do not wish to spend a lot of time, you can just add a small section or even one row at the bottom of the front panel.

To begin a long-stitch sample, first cast on, attach the comb and weights, and knit at least one row with the carriage. The yarn used to knit long stitches can be placed through the tension unit or on the floor in front of you. If you choose to use the yarn in your tension unit, remove it from the yarn feeder.

1. Pull needles that you want to make long stitches all the way out; it can be the entire row or smaller sections of a row.

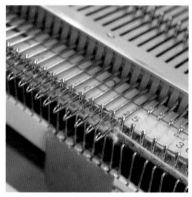

2. Slowly push the needles back, just enough so that the latches are aligned with the pegs. Make sure that the latches remain open.

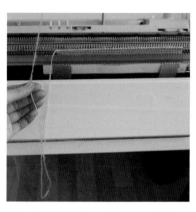

3. Lay the yarn on top of the open latches. Manually pull it from the cone and hold a loose tension with your hand.

4. Push the needles back without completing the stitch, just enough so that the latches close and trap the yarn.

5. Holding a loose tension, manually knit pulling stitches one at a time all the way to the back or however long you would like your stitches to be.

6. Carefully pull the comb downwards so that the needles go in the normal working position and repeat the process.

Simple long-stitch rows can be combined with sections knitted in stockinette stitch, which will also give more structure to the fabric. Before knitting rows with the carriage, pull the needles all the way out.

If you feel a lot of resistance when pulling the needle to the back and the previous long stitches are being pulled and shortened or the row becomes uneven, it might mean that the needles were pushed too far back on Step 3. In case that happens, pull the needles gently towards you and try again; if the issue persists it might mean that the yarn has got caught in one of the needles.

When manually knitting stitches, the end of the yarn is taken out of the yarn feeder and moved to the opposite side of where the carriage is. If you want to use the carriage to knit rows after completing the long-stitch row, you must move the carriage across without knitting. To do so, you can pass the carriage across right after pulling the long stitch as needles are in non-working position. Another option is to put the carriage in holding position after you complete Step 1, as the needles are in holding position as well, and move it to the other side without knitting.

Long stitches can be manipulated in different ways: they can be transferred, twisted or crossed. Creating fabrics this way is laborious and can be time-consuming, but the result is worth the work required. By using the right yarns, you can create luxurious lace fabrics with these stitches and techniques. I knew from the moment I learnt these techniques that I wanted to use them to make my own wedding dress.

In this sample, I knitted one long-stitch row followed by 2 rows knitted with the main carriage.

MANIPULATING LONG STITCHES

Crossing

The first hand-manipulation we will explore is crossing long stitches; if you are familiar with cables, you will find this to be a very similar technique. You will use things you have learnt in Chapter 1, such as how to pick up stitches with the transfer tool and transfer them.

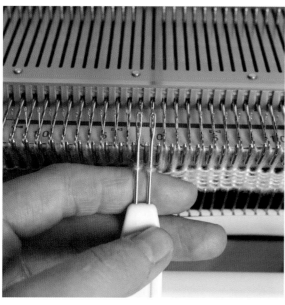

Following the steps shown earlier, knit one long-stitch row. Then, using a 2-prong tool, pick 2 stitches and hold them on your tool.

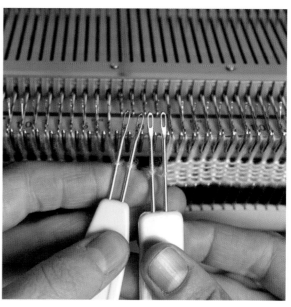

Hold the tool you used before with one hand and pick up 2 more stitches using a second 2-prong tool. Now you will have 4 stitches picked up in total.

Move all the stitches to the left and place the stitches that were on the right-hand side on the needles on the left-hand side like so.

Place the remaining 2 stitches on the empty needles. It is quite difficult to explain this; I like to think that the stitches are just swapping places.

The entire row completed. You can choose to cross a different number of long stitches, knit a few rows of stockinette stitch in between or continue creating long stitches and crossing them on every row.

Charting long crossed stitches

If you want to develop designs with long crossed stitches, just like regular stitches you can use squared paper to draw your designs or plan patterns. There are not any special symbols for these stitches, or at least I have not been able to find any, so I invented some myself. I just draw every stitch as a line over 3 squares on the paper to emphasise that they are long. A square horizontally is a stitch, but 3 squares vertically will be one row.

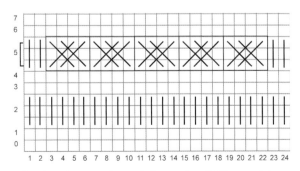

In this chart there are 2 long-stitch rows: 2 and 5. The remaining rows before, in between, and after are regular rows knitted with the carriage.

Twisting

Twisting stitches is another fun method you can use for your samples; this is a technique that can be used for regular stitches as well. You can twist up to 3 stitches at once; more than that and the fabric gets distorted – but that might be an effect that you want to create. You will need to use a type of yarn that is strong enough to be able to twist normal stitches.

Knit one long-stitch row; pick up 2 chosen stitches and place them on your 2-prong tool. You can pick up a different number of stitches.

You are now ready to twist the stitches; in this example I will twist them to the left so I will begin by lifting the opposite end of the tool as shown.

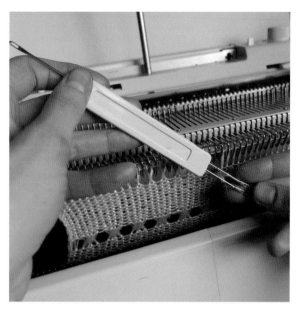

Continue with the round motion to complete the twist (imagine you are drawing a circle with the end of the tool). In this example I twisted the stitches once and I placed them back on their original needles.

An entire row of twisted stitches completed. You can even twist one long stitch at a time to create a more defined long-stitch row.

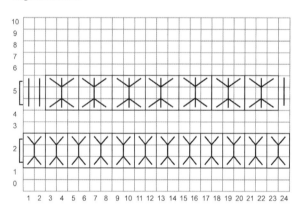

These are the symbols I have been using to represent long twisted stitches in a chart; the second row shows 2 twisted stitches and row 5 shows 3 twisted stitches.

Transferring

In Chapter 1 you learnt how to transfer stitches to create eyelets. In the same way, you can also transfer long stitches: pick up a stitch using your tool and place it on another needle. The outcome is slightly different as the eyelets are also elongated; to me it looks a little bit like crochet, especially in the pattern demonstrated next.

To make the process of transferring 2 stitches on the same needle a little bit faster, first pick up the stitch next to the centre needle and before transferring it, pick up the next one and transfer them both at once onto the centre needle.

You can spend some time developing other samples inspired by this design, this is just one idea – the options are endless. Make sure to create a chart

Choose a centre needle, transfer one stitch on either side; now the centre needle has 3 stitches, and there are 2 empty needles.

Transfer 2 more stitches so that the centre needle has 5 stitches; now there are 2 empty needles on either side.

This is how an entire row looks at this stage; in between every section with transfers, leave one long stitch.

Pull the needle that has 5 stitches all the way out and place the 2 needles closest to it back in action, leave the other 2 out of work and knit 2 rows.

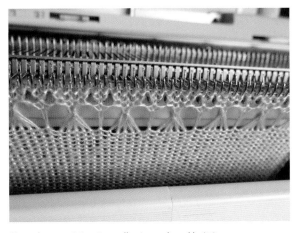

Place the remaining 2 needles in work and knit 2 more rows; you have now completed one repeat. To begin a new repeat, knit another long-stitch row and repeat the process.

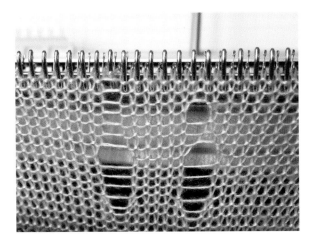

and write down your instructions or take photos along the way to have a record of the steps taken.

In Step 4, the reason why we are placing the needles in action one at a time is because the machine is not able to cast on to 2 empty needles at once.

To make the sample demonstrated above a little bit different, you can stagger the transfers. This can

In both examples in the image, I have transferred to empty 2 needles like the sample shown previously. After knitting a few rows, I placed both needles at once in work on the left-hand side, and one at a time on the right-hand side. This is what happens when placing both needles at once in action and knit rows. The stitches are not casting on and a 2-needle ladder continues to be formed instead.

be a great way to develop different variations of a particular design and make it more interesting. You must plan your pattern beforehand; for example, this repeat will only work when you have an odd number of stitches. To do variations of this design you can try having 3 or even 7 stitches instead of 5 on that needle.

☐ - purl

▨ - ladder (the needle stays in non-working position)

◎ - eyelet (the needle goes back in working position)

- five long stitches onto one needle

- long stitch row (row 2, 6 and 10 are long stitch rows)

The repeat in line.

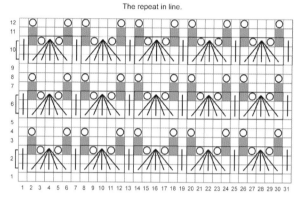

The repeat staggered.

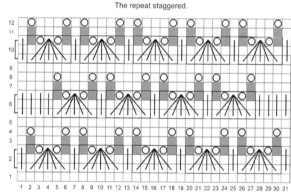

Charts for the 2 stitches. I find it easier to first draw the box and then the long stitches inside. Once I have the 5 stitches area marked, it is simple to see where the centre one is and use that to guide me to draw the rest of the symbols. I left the stitch in between outside the box; this way I found it easier to centre the box for the next staggered row.

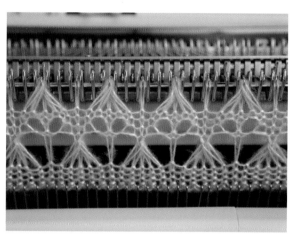

I have completed one repeat just as in the sample shown earlier, and for the next row, I alternated the transfers. The needle that previously had 5 stitches will now have only one and vice versa.

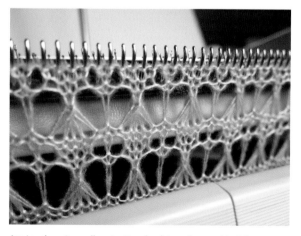

Again, place 2 needles at a time back in action and knit 2 rows in between. This will now be one repeat of the pattern completed. To start a new repeat, continue as per the first row.

In the next long-stitch design, you will learn how to manually cast on when transferring and emptying multiple needles. You can do the transfers gradually by emptying one needle at a time or transfer multiple stitches at once. You can cast on stitches instead of placing them in action one at a time if you do not want so much openness in your fabric. Use a stronger yarn for this sample, as you will have to transfer across multiple stitches which may cause yarns to snap.

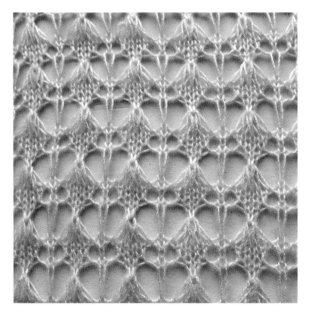
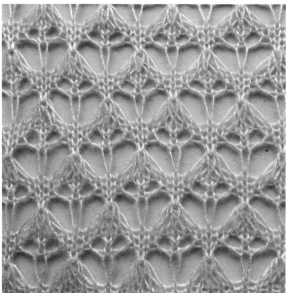

The sample on the left has the transfer repeat in line; on the right is the sample with the design repeated staggered. This is a good example of how staggering the repeat can make the same stitch look different.

Using a 3-prong tool, transfer three stitches at once to the right, pulling the needles out as you complete the transfer; all three needles on the right will have two stitches. When finishing transferring across, you will have three needles in work and three out of work .

Pull the needles with 2 stitches all the way out (if you haven't done this when completing the transfer) and manually knit a long-stitch row; you will have 3 long stitches with a ladder in between. You can choose to knit rows with the carriage for a different outcome.

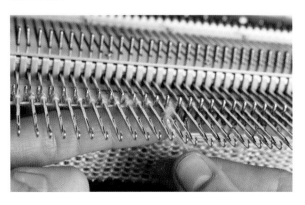

LEFT: Bring all the needles forward again and e-wrap in the same way as you would to begin a new sample. I make sure to always knit the long-stitch row from right to left so I can e-wrap from left to right.

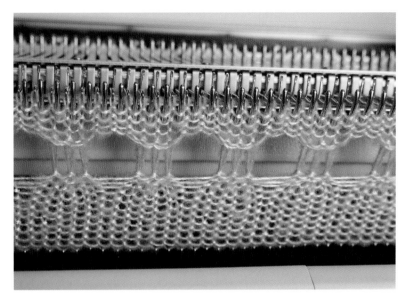

You can now knit as many rows as you would like with the carriage, and you have completed one repeat. To continue with a new repeat, transfer over 3 to empty the same 3 needles we emptied before, but to the left this time and keep alternating with every transfer. We must alternate the direction of the transfer to even out the fabric.

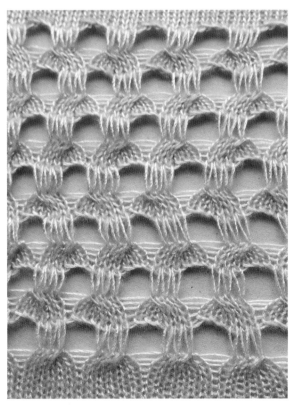

For this sample, I have knitted 4 rows after e-wrapping.

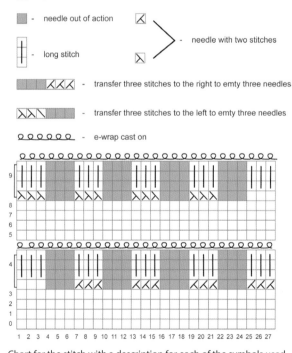

Chart for the stitch with a description for each of the symbols used.

Tuck stitch

It was hard to decide where to include the tuck stitch in the book – the long-stitch chapter ended up feeling like the right place. A tuck stitch is created when a needle that has a stitch receives one or more loops on top of that stitch. Most knitting machines have tucking cams that will enable you to knit tuck patterns with the carriage using the punch-card or by selecting needles manually. For the Brother, if you press the right tuck cam, the carriage will tuck when knitting from right to left. When the left tuck cam is pressed it will tuck when knitting from left to right. By pressing both cams, the carriage will tuck in both directions.

The method we will explore next uses the holding position to accumulate tucks and elongate stitches.

Use a 5/1 needle pusher to bring forward, or into 'E' position, one needle in every 5 and knit 4 rows.

This is a very easy technique to create more subtle open sections, but it can also be combined with ladders and eyelets for a more open effect. To begin the sample demonstrated, set the carriage to hold; refer to the manual to learn how to set the carriage to hold for your machine. When knitting tucks, use a little bit more weight than you would usually; for this sample I have 50 needles in work while using 2 claw weights which I will move up as I knit, plus one small ribber bed weight which will stay on the comb.

The number of rows you can knit or the number of tucks a needle can accumulate will depend on how many needles are in between the ones on hold, the yarn and the tension you are using. If you knit too many rows, the stitches adjacent to the needle placed on hold might not knit properly and cause irregularities or unwanted tucks. On the other hand, if you do not knit enough rows the effect achieved might not be noticeable enough. The held stitch needs to become sufficiently elongated if you want to get the 2 little holes on either side of it.

You must spend some time experimenting to see what works, which is always part of the process. If you want to create bolder and more open patterns you can combine tuck stitches with ladders, eyelets and long stitches.

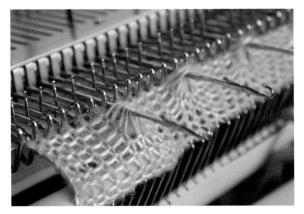

After knitting the 4 rows, only the 5 needles in between completed a stitch; the ones pushed out have accumulated 4 tucks.

Push these needles back in work; for my machine it is enough to push them about halfway in, to knit on the next row. The carriage stays in holding position.

Using the needle pusher, again bring out one needle every 5 but this time, push the needles right in the centre of the previous repeat and knit 4 more rows.

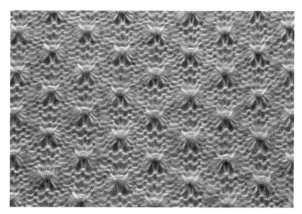

This is the purl side of the swatch. The texture is more obvious on the purl side so you might consider using this as the right side of your project.

In this example I have transferred a stitch on either side of the needles that will be placed on hold. I used the needle pusher to first bring them slightly forward first, which helped me see which stitches I needed to transfer.

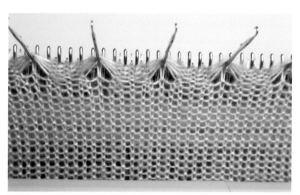

The needles I emptied are left in non-working position followed by knitting 6 rows. That will create a ladder on either side of the needle on hold and will elongate the tucks. Having ladders also enables you to knit more rows to accumulate more tucks.

The next step is to place the needles that were on hold in work and knit one row; I find it easier to leave the carriage on hold during the entire sample and manually put needles in work instead of remembering to keep changing the setting on the carriage.

Just as in the previous example, the repeats are alternated. Transfer a stitch on either side of the needles going on hold next. The stitches will be transferred onto the needles emptied previously and will stop the ladders we created from forming.

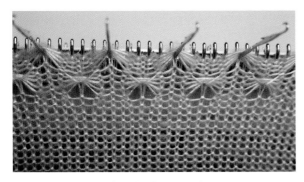

Knit 6 rows and repeat from the first row to begin a new repeat. This might seem like a very complicated pattern, but as soon as you practise a couple of repeats it will seem more straightforward.

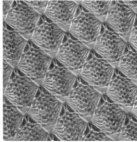

On the left-hand side is the sample with the knit side uppermost; on the right-hand side is the sample showing the purl side.

Charting tuck stitches

The tuck stitch symbol looks like an upside-down upper-case letter 'U'. The tuck symbol shows for how many rows the needle was left on hold and you can see how many tucks it accumulated by simply counting these rows. It would be quite difficult to draw every single tuck accumulated on the needle and to create a clear chart.

☐ - purl   ⊓ - needle with four tucks

This is the chart for the first tuck stitch sample shown previously. The tuck symbol looks elongated to show that the needle accumulated 4 tucks or was placed on hold for 4 rows.

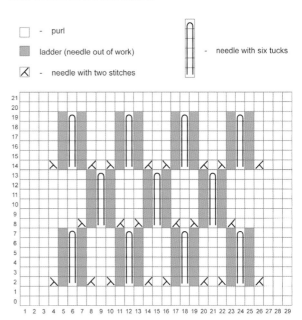

☐ - purl

▨ ladder (needle out of work)

◿ - needle with two stitches

⊓ - needle with six tucks

The chart for the second, more complex sample

ADDING BEADS TO KNIT

If you think manipulating long stitches is fun, you should try adding beads as well. You could also combine them: manipulate stitches and then add beads, or add beads and then manipulate stitches. By adding beads to knitting you can create even more luxurious garments and accessories.

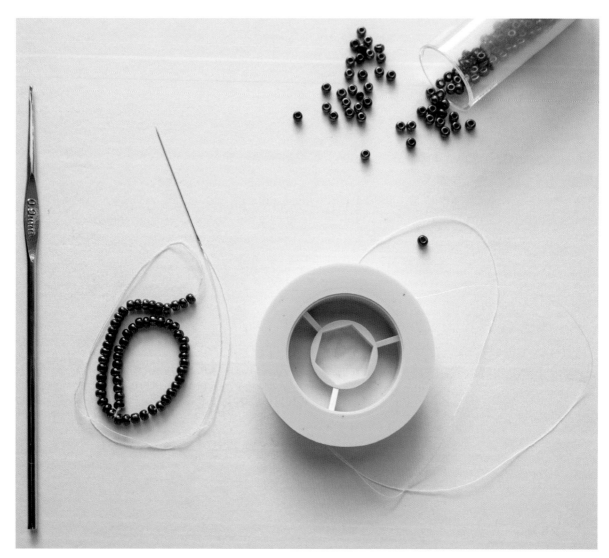

These are the materials you will need to incorporate beads into your knitted sample: beads, a strong thread or very fine yarn, beading needle (or any needle that can fit through the hole in your bead), and a small crochet hook for larger beads.

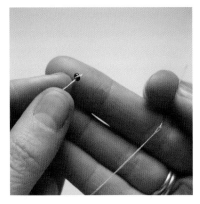

1. Thread your needle with a strong thread and secure the end with a bead or a larger knot. The thread should not be too long otherwise it might get tangled.

2. Load your beads; you have secured the end so the beads will not fall off. You can decide at this point if you want them in a specific order according to colour.

3. Knit a long-stitch row. Use a 1-prong tool to pick up a stitch and place the beading needle through the stitch.

4. Pull the thread through so that the stitch is about midway; the thread will hold the stitch and not allow it to run.

5. Place the needle through the last 3 beads loaded on the thread and slide them onto the stitch. Depending on their size, you could slide more or fewer beads.

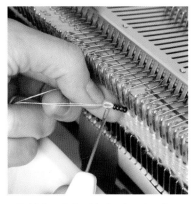

6. Hold the stitch with the thread and use a tool to transfer it back onto its needle. Once the stitch is transferred, pull the thread and let the needle slide off.

A row of beads completed; you could continue with another long-stitch row or knit rows with the carriage. Remember to pull the needle all the way out first.

Make sure to not load too many beads onto one needle so you don't jam the carriage; you should be able to easily place the tool onto the stitch before transferring back on its needle. If you feel resistance, it is a good idea to remove one of the beads or use smaller ones.

As mentioned above, you can also place one bead on 2 or even 3 stitches at once. This can be a little bit trickier so make sure you practise and get comfortable with placing one bead beforehand. A finer yarn will work best; if the yarn is too chunky there is a risk of the stitches not fitting through the hole in the bead. Spend some time practising and finding out what works for the beads and yarn you are using.

As this technique is very laborious and time consuming, you might choose to add beads as a detail in a small section of a garment. Of course, you can experiment and embellish an entire garment or accessory with beads – if you want to try, planning your sample might be useful.

If you have beads of differing colours, you can plan a more intricate motif and create a piece of art. You can start developing it on squared paper by hand or on your laptop. Once you are happy with the design, you may load the beads in the specific colour order and follow the chart to ensure that every row is correct.

Pick up 3 long stitches; place the needle through all 3 and slide the beads on. If you feel too much resistance, try with 2 stitches or larger beads.

Carefully separate the 3 stitches and place them back on their needles. Don't worry if a stitch does not go back on its original needle.

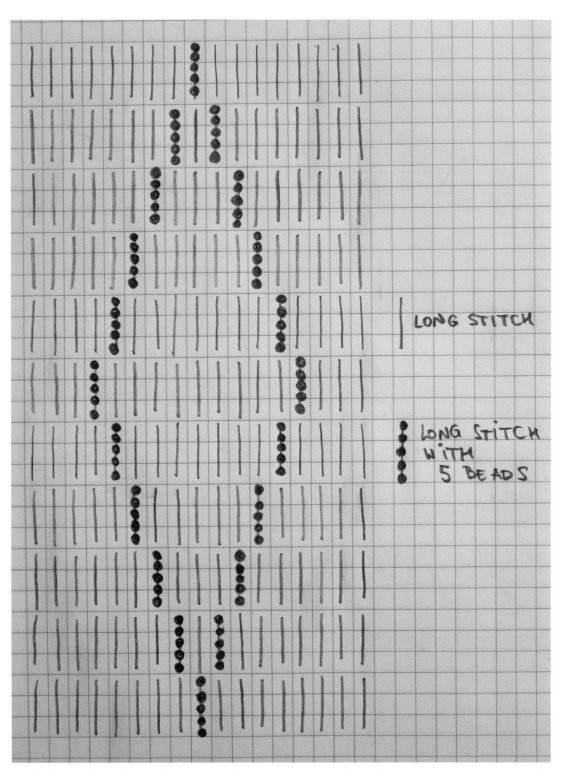

LONG STITCH

LONG STITCH
WITH
5 BEADS

Drawing by hand is a great option to plan your beads' placement. If you want to use different colour beads you can draw and plan that on squared paper as well. The sample with long stitches with beads is shown overleaf.

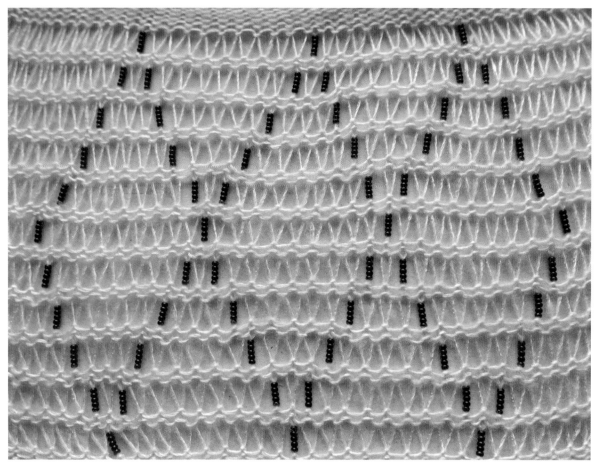

In this example you can see a combination of beaded sections with long stitches in an Argyle shape.

Knit or purl?

Usually, the purl side of the fabric is considered the wrong side, but of course that is your call to make. I often find that I prefer the purl side of a long-stitch design. If you would like to use the purl side of a long-stitch design as the right side of the fabric, or to combine it with different stitches that look better on the knit side, once you finish the long-stitch section knit at least one row with the carriage followed by a few rows in waste yarn, ideally in a contrast colour.

The next step is to remove the entire sample from the machine by dropping the stitches, flip it so that the knit side of the long-stitch section is facing you, and hook it back on the needles. After doing that you can knit as many rows as you like in the other stitch, and then repeat the process by knitting waste yarn, dropping stitches, and re-hooking the sample. This might be time-consuming, but the result is worth it. You can do this much faster if you have a garter bar.

USING LONG-STITCH OR BEADED FABRIC FOR GARMENTS

Measuring samples

Despite not having an accurate row count as we are not using the carriage for every row, it is not difficult to plan projects with long stitches or beaded fabrics. I usually like to knit a tension swatch and make a note of how many stitches and repeats I have completed. These repeats can be a combination of rows knitted with the carriage and long-stitch rows in between, or long-stitch rows only. I will knit my sample, steam it and/or wash it, measure it, and plan my garment according to the size of that swatch. Again, we are working backwards, just as in the example in Chapter 1. When knitting, I like to write down how many repeats I must do and tick each one off once I complete it, to keep track of where I am.

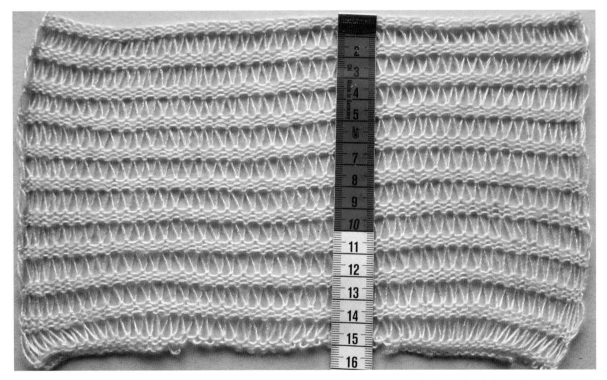

This sample is 50 stitches and 10 repeats (or rows): a repeat is formed of one long-stitch row with 2 knitted with the carriage. It is 27cm wide and 15cm long – I can now divide these numbers to find my gauge and calculate to plan the project I would like to make.

KNITTING TIPS

- To avoid moving the carriage across to where the yarn end is after manually knitting a long-stitch row, you can just use 2 cones of yarn; one fed through the yarn tension unit to use for knitting rows with the carriage, and one on the floor in front of you to use for knitting the manual rows.

- If you haven't got them already, it's a good idea to obtain some needle pushers in different combinations. They make your life easier, especially when bringing needles forward for different patterns.
- Using plied-up yarn can reduce how well you can see the details in a long-stitch design. Test the yarns before starting a project: wash and steam to see how the yarn behaves.

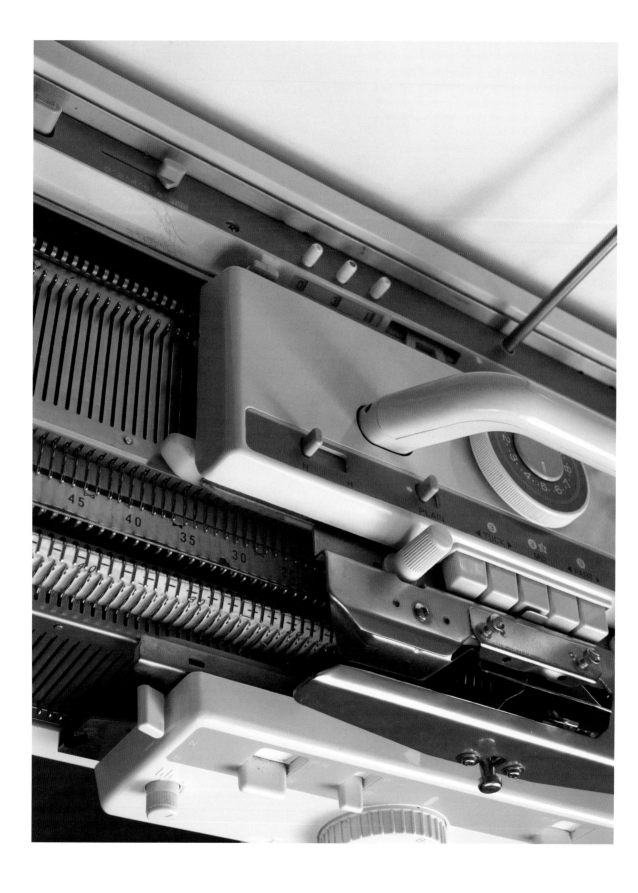

CHAPTER 4

DOUBLE-BED OPEN FABRICS

n this chapter I will share some ideas you can use to create open knit fabrics on a double bed. You will learn how to create simple long stitches in a faster way, some lace knit-purl designs and some ideas on how you can add details to your rib trims.

DOUBLE-BED KNITTING

To use the lace techniques demonstrated in this chapter you will need a ribber bed. The ribber bed will enable you to automatically produce both knit and purl stitches in the same row. When you transfer a stitch from main bed to ribber bed, that stitch will become a purl stitch on the knit side and vice versa. You can also produce purl stitches on the knit side on a single bed by forming a ladder and then using a latch tool to manually reform these stitches.

Buying my ribber bed was one the best decisions that I have made. It helped me to take my machine knitting skills to the next level and opened a whole new world of possibilities. Besides the creative potential, the ribber bed will enable you to create professional and beautifully finished projects by adding rib trims and necklines. When you add ribbing at the bottom of a sample, it will prevent it from curling, even without being blocked.

I will be the first to admit that I found it a little bit intimidating at first and that it took me a while to get used to all the functions but, as with everything, the more I practised, the more comfortable I became using it.

Beds pitch

The beds pitch refers to the alignment of the beds, which ultimately impacts the alignment of the needles of the main bed with the ones of ribber bed. You must have beds in full pitch when knitting any type of rib: 1×1, 2×2 and so forth. The beds must be in half pitch when knitting a full needle rib or when knitting a design that requires you to have all needles in work on the ribber bed, and any needle formation on the main bed.

Half-pitch lever on the Brother. This is found on the left side of the ribber bed, next to the racking grip handle. When the lever is set to 'P', beds are in full pitch. When the lever is set to 'H', the beds are in half pitch.

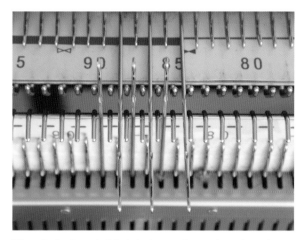

When the beds are in full pitch, the needles on the main and ribber bed are directly opposite each other. Therefore, the needles must be alternated when they are in work so that they do not crash into each other.

When beds are in half pitch, the placement of the needles is alternated – they can cross without colliding. In half pitch, you can have all the needles in work at the same time.

Weights and tension

You need to use more weights when knitting on a double bed rather than a single. When switching between single and double bed, make sure to adjust the weights accordingly.

As the stitches' loops become longer, the tension must be reduced and, as always, you will have to test your tension depending on yarn and stitch.

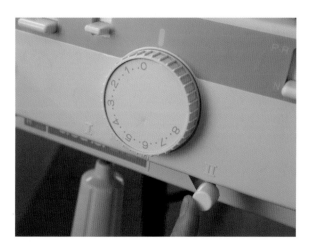

To knit at an even tighter tension than 0 on the ribber bed, you can move the lever on the carriage from 'I' to 'II'. You are most likely to need to do that when casting on your ribbing.

LONG STITCH ON A DOUBLE BED

If you have a ribber bed, creating long (also known as dropped) stitches can be much easier and quicker. When using this method, there are a few limitations: the stitches will be a little shorter than when they are knitted manually, and it might impact how you can manipulate them. In Chapter 5, we will explore how producing long stitches manually will give you more freedom when it comes to the yarn that can be used. However, it is still worth spending some time practising as you might prefer slightly shorter stitches. This is still a great learning opportunity, and it will give you some ideas.

I usually leave the needles in action on the ribber bed for the entire sample and set the ribber carriage so that it doesn't knit, instead of putting needles in and out of work while I knit rows on the main bed only. On the Brother, place the knobs in 'PR' position. Test a sample so that all the steps make sense and see what works best for you.

If you want to create larger sections of long stitches without any rows knitted on the main bed only, repeat the third step as many times as you want and drop the stitches on the ribber bed on the last row. This will save you a bit of time, as the rows knitted before will unravel all at once revealing the long stitches up to the point where you knitted the first row on both beds. Depending on the yarn you are using, the carriage might move across with difficulty, so doing it one row at a time will be the better option. Make sure you are using a strong yarn when doing this; I had a few accidents using older lambswool and my yarn snapped.

1. Cast on a sample. If you chose to knit a rib first, once finished, transfer all the stitches from ribber bed to main bed and knit one row on the main bed, just to get an even tension.

2. Make sure the beds are in half pitch and put all the needles in action on the ribber bed. I also like to pull them all the way out or into 'E' position before knitting rows.

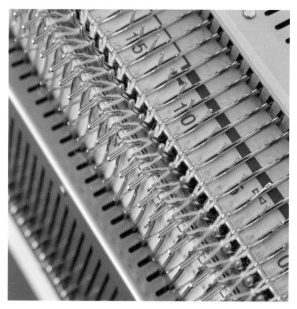

3. Knit one row with all needles in working position. I try to use the loosest tension on the ribber bed so that the stitches are the longest possible. It is always important to test and see what works best.

4. Drop all stitches on the ribber bed by moving the carriage on its own across and returning it back to the main carriage. On the Brother, press the little metal knob downwards to release the ribber carriage.

For this sample I knitted one row and dropped the stitches as shown, followed by 2 rows knitted on the main bed only in between. The 2 rows can serve as a design feature but will also give the fabric more structure.

This is another way to produce different patterns with double-bed long-stitch swatches. In this example, there are 5 needles in action and 5 out of action across the ribber bed. You can choose different numbers of needles.

Knit one row with all needles in action then drop the stitches on the ribber bed. Only the needles placed in action on the ribber bed will knit. Make sure to go across slowly; this might feel a little bumpy.

For the next row, the needles that were in action in the previous row will stay out of action and vice versa. The needles must be alternated so that the fabric evens out, but it will also make the long stitches more obvious.

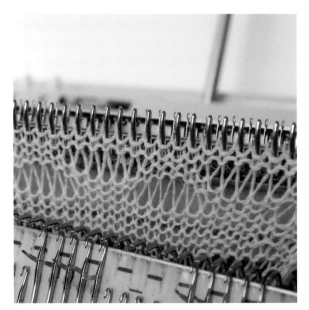

In this example I knitted 2 rows on the main bed in between the dropped stitch rows. This is one long-stitch design where I prefer the look of the purl side of the fabric to the knit side.

Scalloped edge

A scalloped edge can easily elevate the look of a knitted garment, making it more special even when the stitch on the body is simple – this is one of my favourite trims. To create a scalloped edge, you must do fully fashioned transfers to create eyelets as shown in Chapter 1, ideally in each row. The transfers are what pull the stitches in and distort the edge of the fabric, so doing this in equal sections will give you a lovely wavy edge. You can of course use this on a single bed and skip the first steps – in Chapter 1, one of the samples shown also had a little scalloped edge because of the transfers. The edge in that sample was curling, but it is possible to produce a neater scalloped edge using the ribber bed to cast on a full-needle rib.

I recommend using a waste yarn cast-on for your projects, which I find always achieves the best edge for my rib. There are a couple of different ways to do a waste yarn cast-on; in the next step-by-step sequence I will show you the method I always use for any ribbing. You can choose to cast on without waste yarn when you want to test designs to make the process a bit quicker.

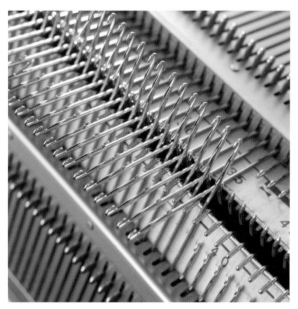

1. Make sure your beds are in half pitch and place all the needles you want to use in action. For this sample I will cast on 70 stitches.

2. Place the waste yarn in the feeder, knit one row on all needles and insert the comb and weights. I will use 2 large ribber bed weights for this sample.

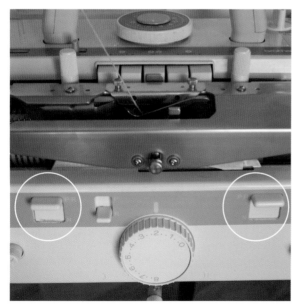

3. Knit a few rows in waste yarn, about 10 rows should be enough, then knit 3 rows on the main bed only. To do that on the Brother I must place the 2 knobs into 'PR' position.

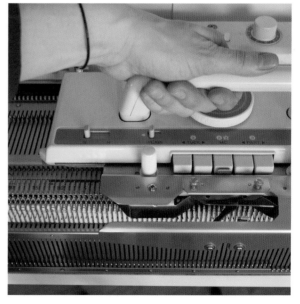

4. Move the knobs on the ribber carriage back to 'N' and knit one row on all needles. Remove the yarn from the feeder and drop all the stitches on the main bed by going across with the main carriage only.

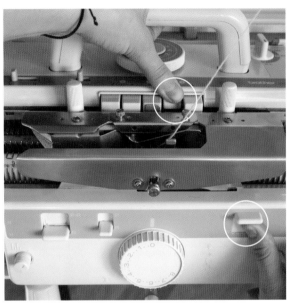

5. Snap your waste yarn, feed your final yarn, and knit one row on all the needles; this is called the cast-on row. Use the tightest tension possible for this row to get a good tight edge.

6. Knit 3 rows tubular. For the Brother I must press the left partial cam on the main bed and place the right knob on the ribber carriage in 'PR' position, or the other way around.

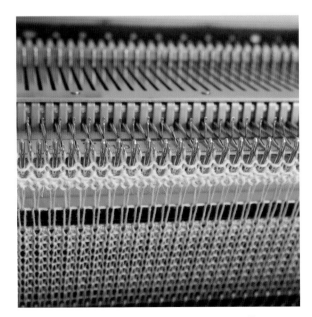

7. Place your carriages back in the normal position and knit one row with all needles. Then transfer all stitches from ribber bed to main bed and knit 2 rows on the main bed only; you are now ready to start fully fashioned transfers.

In this example, you will do 2 repeats of transfers using a 3-prong tool every one row. From now you can continue with any design you like, or even leave the rest of the sample in stockinette stitch.

The sample taken off the machine with waste yarn still attached. Stitches are neat and not stretched out because I used a waste yarn cast-on. To remove the waste yarn, snap the last loop and pull the tail to unravel the entire row.

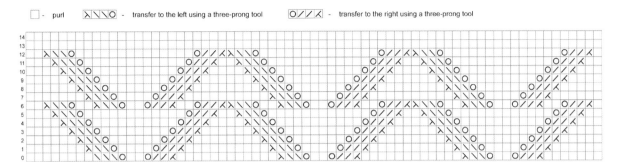

This is the chart for this sample. I only included the repeat for the scallop, as you might choose to do a different type of cast-on.

Knitting one row in between every fully fashioned transfer and moving one stitch further (to the left or to the right) with every transfer is what will pull the stitches and distort the fabric. To add a little extra detail at the edge of your scallops, after knitting the first 2 rows on the main bed, you can transfer the stitches back onto the ribber, knit 2 rows and then transfer them back on the main bed. That will add a couple of purl stitches embellishing the edge.

If this is the first time you have seen a full needle waste yarn cast-on, you might think that there are too many steps and that you will never remember them. Follow these steps a few times, practise them, and you will be able to do them without thinking, ready to use this cast-on method for a bigger project. It is easy to experiment with complex projects before being ready and end up feeling discouraged when unsuccessful – it rarely works the first time, and that is fine. It is all part of the learning process.

It will depend on the yarn you are using if a waste yarn cast-on is necessary or not. Use a waste yarn cast-on if the yarn used is fine or fragile, or if you want to start a design that involves transfers right after or very close to the cast-on row. Using a waste yarn cast-on will produce a neater outcome.

Charts for a double bed

When developing designs for a double bed on squared paper, you can use the same symbols you have learnt in Chapter 1. I will introduce 2 symbols found in double-bed stitch charts: the purl stitch symbol that will show which needles are in action on the ribber bed, and the arrow symbol which shows on which row a transfer between beds takes place. There are a couple of ways I have been using to represent a purl stitch in a chart:

Option 1 – In this chart the square in which there is a vertical line represents a knit stitch and the square in which there is a horizontal line represents a purl stitch; that means that if you follow this chart, you will produce a 1×1 ribbing.

Option 2 – In this chart every square drawn in grey is a knit stitch and every square left in white is a purl stitch. This is the method I personally use and find to be the easiest. Follow this chart to produce a 2×2 ribbing.

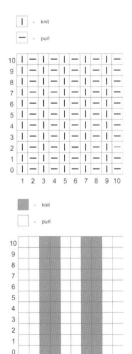

The sample produced by following the chart.

If a stitch is transferred from main bed to ribber bed, the 'arrow pointing downwards' symbol is used and if a stitch is transferred from ribber bed to main bed, we use the 'arrow pointing upwards' symbol. Using 2 colours is very useful when doing transfers from one bed to the other.

When knitting fabrics on the double bed, I usually like to do transfers or any other manipulation on the main bed as I find this is the most comfortable. That means that when the sample hangs on the machine, the wrong side of the fabric is facing me. I know some machine knitters who prefer doing transfers on the ribber bed as they find that easier; that means that the right side of the fabric is facing them. You might need to consider this when creating your charts but remember that there is not a wrong or right way, just find what is easiest for you. The same applies for the charts. You might even want to create your own symbols; there are no rules if it will make your life easier.

Incorporating lace holes in rib trims

I am a big fan of small but clever details in knitwear. Some of these details are discussed in Chapter 1, such as the way a garment is constructed, and of course trims. Over the last couple of years, I have started adding cables, transfers and eyelets to my trims; there are so many ways you can make a simple standard 1×1 or 2×2 rib more exciting by adding some simple lace holes. I will share some ideas that I hope will inspire you to practise and spend time developing designs of your own. But first, I will demonstrate how to cast on a 1×1 rib without waste yarn. If you want to do a waste yarn cast-on, follow the same steps demonstrated for the scalloped edge shown earlier in the chapter up to Step 4.

☐ - purl (needle in action on main bed)

▨ - knit (needle in action on ribber bed)

⤓ - needle transferred from main to ribber bed

⤒ - needle transferred from ribber to main bed

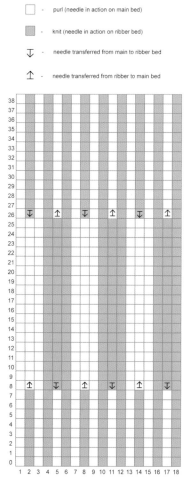

If you follow this chart, you will begin with a 1×1 ribbing. On row 8, stitches 2, 8 and 14 are transferred from ribber bed to main bed; stitch 5, 11 and 17 are transferred from main to ribber bed. From row 9–26 we will produce a 3×3 ribbing. On row 26, stitches 2, 8, and 14 are transferred from main to ribber bed and stitches 5, 11 and 17 are transferred from ribber to main bed. We are producing again a 1×1 ribbing from row 27–38.

1. Make sure your beds are in full pitch and, using a needle pusher, place in work as many needles as you would like to use. In this example, my ribbing is over 50 needles.

2. Knit one row and insert your comb and weights; 2 large weights should be enough. Knit this row at the tightest tension the yarn you are using will allow.

3. Knit 3 rows tubular to complete the cast-on. Trims always take a few tries to get right so testing the tension is very important.

4. Return both carriages back to normal and knit the 1×1 rib. If you would like to do transfers after the first rows you might want to do a waste yarn cast-on as shown earlier in the chapter.

When practising and testing this design, it is better to begin with a looser tension to avoid any problems, and then tightening after you have done a few transfers (if the yarn will allow you to). As the transfers are done over 2 needles rather than just one, this can cause a lot of extra tension and there is a risk of the yarn snapping. You can knit the rows where there are transfers at a tighter tension and increase it for the rows with transfers. Also, be extra careful when a needle has 2 or more stitches; to be safe, pull that needle all the way out before knitting rows to ensure that the stitch is completed properly.

I will demonstrate transfers row-by-row so you can give these designs a try and use them in one of your future projects. When counting the needles, I will only include needles that have a stitch or are in work.

Design idea 1 – 1×1 ribbing with eyelets

Start counting from the left-hand side, skip 2 needles from the edge and, using a 1-prong tool, transfer the third stitch on the next working needle. Imagine that you jump over the needle that is out of work.

Take the fifth stitch and transfer onto the next working needle on the left. Now the fourth needle has 3 stitches. If you feel too much resistance, stop, knit a couple more rows at a looser tension and try again.

The squares drawn in white are purl stitches, or needles in action on the main bed. The squares in grey are knit stitches or needles in action on the ribber bed. Again, imagine that when you look at the chart, you see the sample as it hangs off the machine. The arrows are showing where to transfer the stitches and the little circle shows the lace hole which will be formed after knitting rows; these symbols are my own invention.

☐ - purl

▨ - knit

[◀─O] - transfer over two needles to the left

[O─▶] - transfer over two needles to the

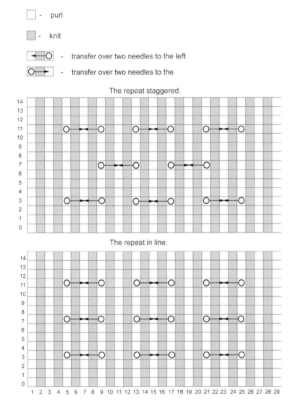

The repeat staggered.

The repeat in line.

Charts for the 2 samples with explanations for every symbol used.

Skip one stitch and continue transferring in the same way across the entire front bed. Use a 1/1 needle pusher to make sure that all needles are in the correct position and knit 4 rows.

For the next row I will alternate the transfers and now the needle I previously skipped will have 3 stitches. You can choose to continue in the same way as the first row.

The sample on the left is a repeat of the first row only; the one on the right has the repeats staggered. I prefer the sample with alternated repeats and how it distorts the stitches.

1. Begin with beds in half pitch and using the 2/2 needle pusher, place 2 needles in work and 2 needles out of work across the main and ribber beds.

2. Knit one row with all needles at the tightest tension, then insert the comb and weights. For this sample I am using 2 large weights.

3. Knit 3 rows tubular. You might need to increase the tension for these 3 rows.

4. Put the beds in full pitch; that will move the ribber bed once to the left. Rotate the racking grip handle so that the ribber bed moves to the left once more.

5. The beds and needles are now in the correct position, and you are ready to knit the 2×2 ribbing.

2×2 ribbing with eyelets and ladders

Next, I will show you a couple of design ideas you can try to incorporate in your next project that has a 2×2 ribbing. Spend some time developing different designs that begin with a 2×2 rib and play with transfers between beds to knit a section of 4×4 or other even number and include more lace holes.

The next sample is a variation of the same design, but this time I did not place the needle I transferred back in action for the next 4 rows.

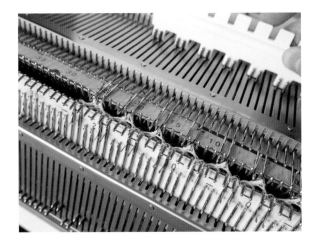

LEFT: In this example, I transferred a stitch on the main bed to form an eyelet and will alternate that every 2 rows. Using a 2/2 needle pusher, I ensure that I place the needles correctly back in action before knitting rows.

BELOW: The knitted sample. I left sections of plain 2×2 ribbing in between the transfers. I really like how that distorts the ribbing.

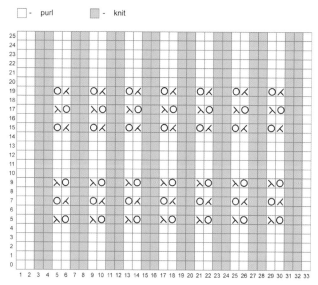

- purl   - knit

☐ - purl   ▨ - knit

Ⓞ - eyelet (needles goes back in working position)

⌣ - ladder (needle stays in non-working position)

⅄⌣ - transfer to the left to form a ladder

⌣⅄ - transfer to the right to form a ladder

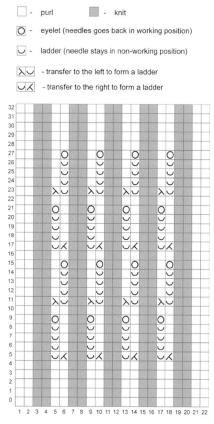

ABOVE: The chart for Version 1 (*see* previous page for sample).

LEFT: Chart for Version 2 with a description for each symbol used (sample below).

BELOW: This produced a ladder. To stop the ladder from forming I simply put the needles back in action. After putting the needle back in action, I knitted 2 more rows and alternated the needle for the next transfer.

TRANSFERS BETWEEN BEDS WITH LACE HOLES

Next, we will explore some knit-purl designs and some ideas to incorporate lace holes between the transfers. Combining fully fashioned transfers with stitch transfers between beds is a great way to create textured fabrics.

You can also transfer stitches in specific patterns and incorporate lace holes to create beautiful fabrics. When transferring bigger sections from the ribber to the main bed you can incorporate larger repeats, such as some of those we have explored in Chapter 1.

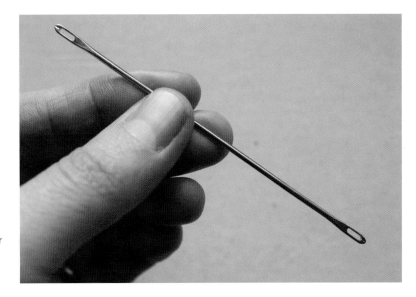

The 2-eye tool is very useful when transferring stitches from main bed to ribber bed. You can use a standard transfer tool if you don't have one; I find that when using the 2-eye tool the process is a bit faster.

Hook one of the eyes, pull the needle and push it back so that the stitch slides on the tool. Lowering the opposite eye of the tool, transfer the stitch onto a needle on the main bed.

To knit this sample, cast on a 1×1 rib then transfer all the needles onto the main bed. First create 4 eyelets by doing fully-fashioned transfers using a 7-prong tool and knitting 2 rows in between. Using the 2-eye tool, transfer all needles to the ribber bed and knit 4 rows. Transfer all needles back onto the main bed and repeat.

This sample begins with a 1×1 ribbing. The next step is to transfer to have a 3×3 rib across and create eyelets as per the chart. To continue, transfer so that the new needle arrangement is 9 needles in work on the main bed, 3 in work on the ribber bed.

- purl

- knit

⼂⼂⼂⼂⼂⼂⼂O - transfer using a seven-prong tool

⬆ - needle transferred from ribber to main bed

⬇ - needle transferred from main to ribber bed

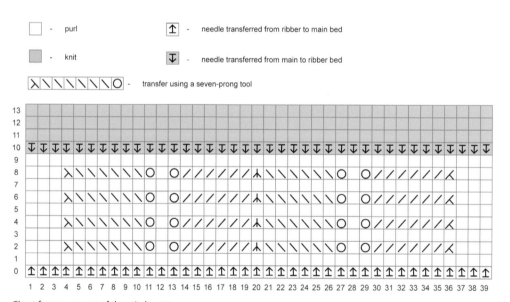

Chart for one repeat of the stitch pattern.

This is the chart for the stitch in this sample.

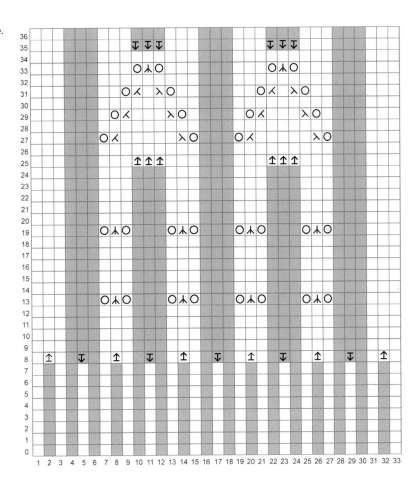

TROUBLESHOOTING

I will focus on a few things that sometimes cause issues on my machine and provide some tips that might help you.

- Knitting rows on the main bed only with the double-bed sinker plate can sometimes cause stitches to tuck, especially on the edges. For example, this can happen if knitting using both beds then transferring all the stitches onto the main bed, continuing to knit on the main bed only. To avoid this happening, make sure to use enough weight and sometimes even pull needles all the way out before knitting rows.

- When knitting larger sections on the main bed only, in between sections knitted on both beds simultaneously, remove some or all of the weights, leaving just the cast-on comb. A good idea is to also change the sinker plate to the single bed one.
- If the tension is too loose when knitting a full-needle rib, the carriage might move across with a lot of difficulty and there is a risk of the yarn snapping if it is fragile. Make sure to go across very slowly when testing and try tightening the tension to see if the issue persists. If that is the case, it might just be the nature of the yarn you are using.

CHAPTER 5

THE MAGIC OF YARN

This chapter is all about experimenting and having fun with yarn; it will look at how yarn impacts the outcome of a lace fabric and different effects we can achieve by combining them. I will take techniques demonstrated in the book and show you how you can make them even more exciting. As much information as possible will be provided about the yarns, such as composition and count.

YARN

Yarn has been mentioned throughout the book without giving specific examples because it is helpful to focus on learning the techniques first. Yarn can easily become a very technical conversation that could fill an entire book; I will briefly discuss some aspects that you might find helpful to start with. All this information is usually written on the label inside the cone.

Knitting yarns can be made of different fibres and materials and can come in a variety of weights and qualities. The most commonly used fibres are animal-based (wool, mohair, cashmere), plant-based (cotton, bamboo, hemp) or man-made synthetic fibres (nylon, polyester, rayon). Yarn can also be made from a blend or a mix of these different fibres

with the purpose of either strengthening it or creating texture.

The weight of a yarn or its count refers to how thick or thin the yarn is. I will not try to explain all the counts, as there are many different units used in different sectors of the textile industry. Even experienced knitters struggle with yarn counts, and rest assured that you will learn and get more confident about this subject in time.

Yarns are produced in many ways; they can be quite simple and clean or more textured and interesting. A few samples in this book have been knitted with yarns more commonly used in the knitwear industry.

Your choice of yarn can add creativity and fun to your designs. I will show you how to experiment with some of the techniques learnt in previous chapters, using novelty or fancy yarns to explore other possibilities. Even when you knit stockinette stitch with some of these yarns, due to their nature you can produce a textured fabric.

It can be quite overwhelming as a beginner to know what yarns are suitable for your knitting machine, so I will try to give you at least a few options when purchasing yarn for the first time. For standard gauge, when you start practising some of the lace techniques demonstrated in this book, a 2ply or a 4ply cotton yarn would be a great start. One of the counts that I use the most is the metric count; in practice, this is the length in metres of 1g of the yarn strand. If 1g of yarn measures 32m, then the metric count of that yarn will be 32 Nm. To show that the yarn has been plied up, the number of plies would be added before the metric count, so if the yarn is plied twice this would be 2/32 Nm. In this chapter you will see a variety of yarns in the metric count and hopefully this will be useful for you when purchasing yarn for your next lace project.

Novelty yarns

Most novelty yarns have a standard yarn as the core and another yarn is either twisted or knotted around it in a specific pattern or at random intervals, to produce loops or other irregularities.

Not every novelty yarn will be suitable for the techniques demonstrated in this book. I will share some of the things I have learnt through trial and error over the years when working with different novelty yarns:

- The more textured a yarn is the less you can see the stitches, something to keep in mind when doing fully fashioned transfers, for example. You can combine them with other yarns to create fun stripes, but the stitches will not be easily visible and in some instances, it will not be worth spending the time to transfer more than one stitch to create the eyelets.
- When creating long stitches using a bouclé yarn, there is a chance that the loops of the yarn will get caught in the needle hooks and make the process difficult or even impossible. However, some bouclé yarns with smaller loops can work beautifully.

A variety of novelty yarn butterflies made from different fibres such as cotton, alpaca, wool, viscose, polyester (bouclé, slub, eyelash, textured tape, knitted sequins, cord).

- It can be quite difficult to transfer when knitting with very textured yarns, such as an eyelash yarn. It does not apply to all eyelash or highly textured yarns, but some do get caught in the latches of the needles, making transfers more difficult.

These are things to consider, but they might not all happen to you, so try and see what works and what does not. If you find that some yarns are just impossible to knit with, you can use them to create fringes or to e-wrap and add an extra detail on the samples that have the purl side as the right side of the fabric (as with the e-wrapping to cast on new stitches for the long-stitch sample in Chapter 3).

Yarn experiment

Lace work can look beautiful in almost any yarn and lace fabrics can be suitable not only for the summer, but also for the colder seasons. In the following images you will see how different the same lace pattern can look when knitted with different yarns. All the swatches have the same number of stitches and same number of rows. I used the lace carriage and a lace pattern from Chapter 2 to knit these samples.

I hope this gives you an insight on how the different yarns used affect the look of a stitch. Perhaps it will inspire you to consider knitting lace with yarns that you previously would not have thought suitable.

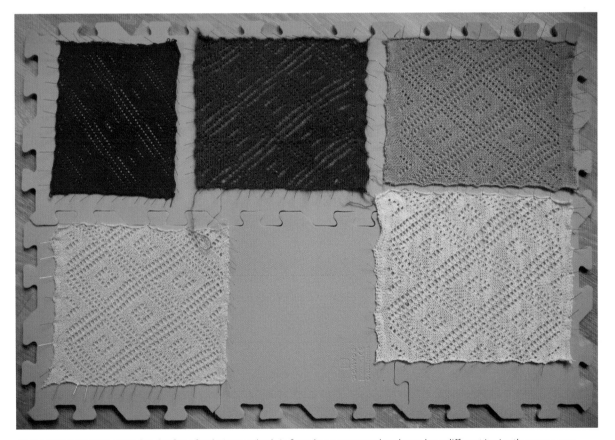

All the swatches were pinned to dry flat, after being washed. At first glance you can already see how different in size they are; some yarns have more stretch than others.

ABOVE LEFT: The yarn used in this sample is cotton slub yarn. A slub is a type of yarn that is thick and thin in random areas of the yarn strand. Yarn information: Nm 3000. Tension used to knit: 10.

ABOVE RIGHT: Cashmere is one of my favourite fibres, as it is very soft, warm and fluffy. Lace holes are still well defined but slightly smaller. For this sample I used 3 ends of 2/28 Nm. Tension used to knit: 8.

LEFT: This is a finer bouclé yarn which gave an attractive textured effect to the lace pattern. It is made from a silk nylon blend, very soft to the touch. Yarn used: 2 ends of 13 Nm/1. Tension used to knit: 5.1.

If you don't want the lace holes to be very well defined, one option would be to use a fluffier yarn such as mohair. Additionally, you can brush it to create a more pronounced fuzzy effect. Yarn used: Nm1000, a blend of mohair, polyamide and wool. Tension used to knit: 5.1.

This sample came out the smallest as the yarn used is very stretchy. You may also notice that the lace holes come out quite small. This is a hand-knitting yarn which also knits nicely on the machine. It is a fingering yarn, and the recommended knitting needle is a 3mm. Tension used to knit: 10.

FULLY FASHIONED TRANSFERS AND STRIPES

When combining fully fashioned transfers and stripes, due to the movement of the stitches, the stripes will become distorted. The number of stitches you transfer when creating the eyelets will impact how much or in what way the stripes will distort. For an even more dramatic effect, knit rows on the ribber bed in between using a different yarn or colour.

Missoni is a fashion brand that uses this technique a lot and the zigzag stripe is their signature; you might have seen their beautiful garments and maybe wondered how they are made. Now you know it is not difficult at all and you could do it too.

In the next sample I combined a few different techniques, such as fully fashioned transfers to create a scalloped edge, rows knitted on the ribber bed and transfers between beds and stripes. Having a small section of simple transfers in a clean yarn balances the design so it is not overwhelming.

You have already seen this lace pattern in Chapter 1, knitted in one colour. When adding more colours and producing stripes, these result in a nice zigzag shape. The properties of the yarn also cause the stripes to be unequal.

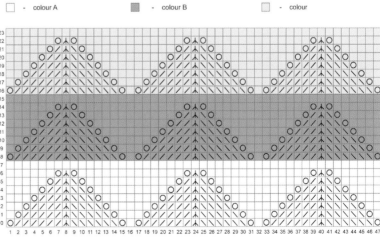

Chart with colour changes. Yarn A – wool, 4 ply. Yarn B – knitted sequins, polyester, Nm 4000. Yarn C – polyacrylic viscose blend, Nm 6000.

This is just an example of how you can combine techniques and stitches learnt throughout the book in one single piece.

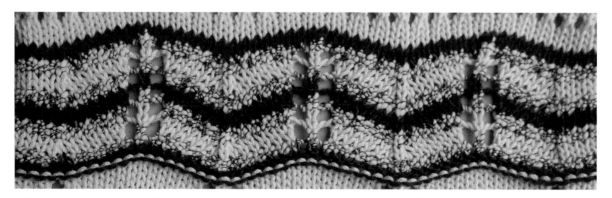

By knitting stripes using yarns with different colours and textures and producing eyelets using fully-fashioned transfers, I achieved a zigzag stripe with an ombre effect.

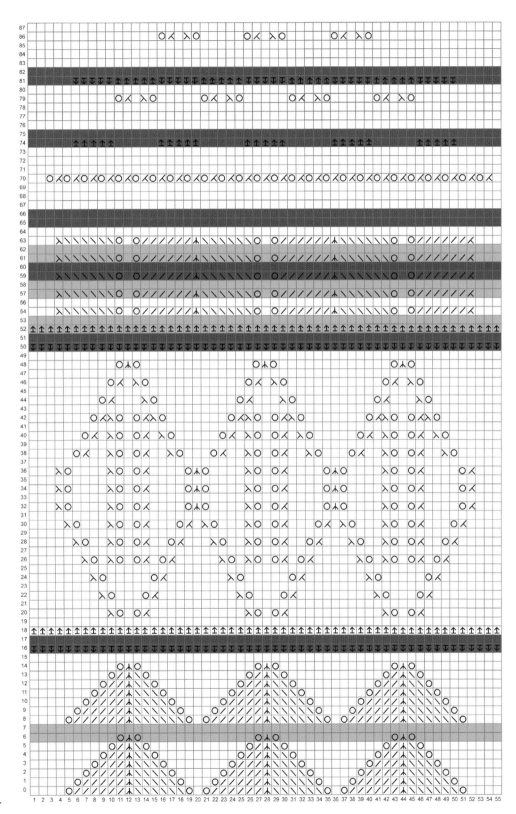

Stitch chart.
Yarn A – 4 ply
mercerised cotton.
Yarn B – acrylic
polyester blend, 3
Nm/1. Yarn C – 2
ply cotton (2 ends).

- colour C
- colour B
- colour A

LONG STITCH

Long-stitch samples look very different to regular stockinette fabric; some long-stitch designs will give the illusion that they are not even knitted. That is something I like about this technique, alongside the multitude of design possibilities. The yarn used has such an important role; you can create a luxurious and special fabric using long stitches.

Using a more textured yarn can reduce the amount of openness that long-stitch fabrics have. In the sample shown next, I have used a fine bouclé yarn and combined long stitches with ladders. Even though

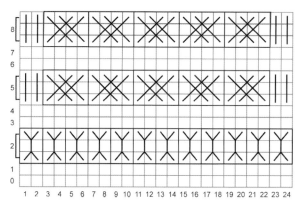

The chart for the stitch. Row 2 shows long twisted stitches, rows 5 and 8 are long crossed stitches. The rest of the rows are knitted with the carriage.

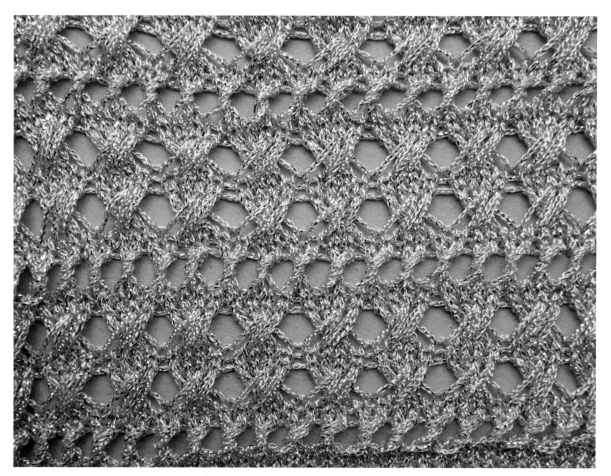

For this sample I combined twisted and crossed long stitches with 2 rows knitted with the carriage in between. The yarn I used is viscose blend, which has a lovely shine and drape. Yarn information: Viscose lurex, 3.8 Nm.

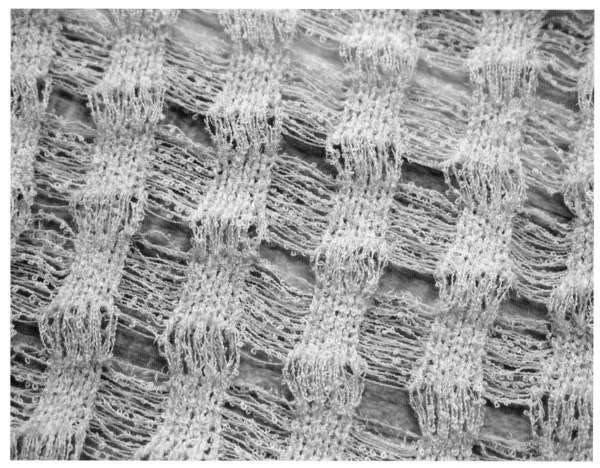

The long stitches are not as obvious when using this textured yarn, but it still creates a nice effect. I knitted the rows with the carriage on a tighter tension than normal.

I have a 4-needle ladder, the texture of the yarn makes the sample less see-through. I had 2 cones of this yarn and alternated between them when knitting rows with the carriage and the rows knitted manually. By doing this I did not need to move my carriage across as one yarn always stayed in the feeder.

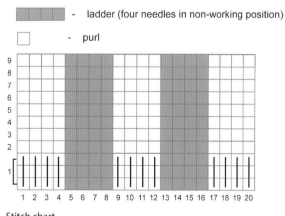

Stitch chart.

When manually knitting long stitches, you can use a hand-knitting yarn or a much chunkier one that you would normally not be able to use on a standard gauge knitting machine. The contrast between the long-stitch rows and the rows knitted with the carriage in a finer yarn will produce a textured effect. This cannot be applied when creating long or dropped stitches with the ribber bed.

When using a chunky yarn, it is even more important to pull the needles all the way out before knitting rows with the carriage to avoid any accidents or breaking needles. This has never happened to me before and hopefully it will not happen to you, but you must be careful. Have a go and try any of the manually knitted long-stitch samples demonstrated in Chapter 3 in a chunkier yarn. To me, these samples resemble crochet.

For this sample I used a ball of 8 ply hand-knitting yarn, which I placed on the floor in front of my machine. The finer one is an eyelash yarn: Nm 1500, 55% cotton, 45% viscose.

I also included some transfers in the sections knitted with the carriage to add more openness; I prefer the purl side of this swatch to be the right side.

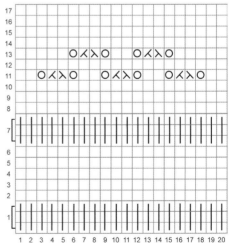

Stitch chart.

Long stitch on a double bed

To make long stitches knitted on a double bed more pronounced, add a second or third colour. As the long-stitch repeat is formed of an odd number of rows, I planned my sample so I did not have the need to snap the yarn at any point or to move the carriage across to where the next colour is. For this sample I used white and 2 shades of blue and, after every row in white, I knitted 2 rows in blue. I tied one of the blue yarns on the left and one on the right side of the machine, so I can swap my colour easily after each row knitted in white.

ABOVE: The yarns that I used for this sample. From left to right: Yarn A: Nm 2/28, 100% cashmere; Yarn B: eyelash yarn made from cotton; Yarn C: fancy tape yarn, cotton polyester blend, 4.6Nm/1.

RIGHT: The purl side of the sample. The colour change is very subtle, but it still creates a beautiful effect.

THREAD LACE

Thread lace or punch lace is an easy technique to create lace or open fabrics using the punch-card. To knit thread lace you must combine 2 yarns of considerably different thicknesses – one very fine and one chunkier – and then knit in the same way as knitting a 2-colour Fair Isle. The stitches knitted with the fine yarn will give the appearance that there are open sections within the fabric. You can even knit using sewing thread or nylon yarn to create some lovely fabrics.

You can use any Fair Isle punch-card you already have or create your own by developing designs on squared paper, as described in Chapter 2. For the punch-cards used to create punch lace there is no need for the blank row, in contrast to the ones used with the lace carriage. The main carriage will roll the card this time and select needles according to your punch-card. These punch-cards will not work with the lace carriage, however, and I would advise you not to try it as it might risk damaging your machine.

This is a pattern which I developed on squared paper; I first drew the shapes and then filled in squares and decided where to punch the holes. This is just an initial design; you can choose to develop it further to your liking.

1. Insert the punch-card in the reader, clip it to form a continuous loop and lock it on row one marked on the card.

2. Set the carriage to 'KC' by rotating the dial and knit one row to select the needles. Only the chunky yarn is placed in feeder 'A' for this row.

3. Knit across to select needles. The carriage is on the right and needles are selected as per row 1 of the punch-card.

4. Unlock the card by moving the button from the circle to the triangle mark in the middle.

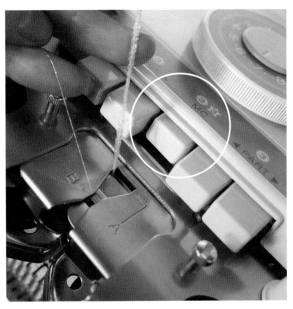

5. Place the fine yarn in feeder 'B' and press the 'MC' cam on the carriage and you are ready to knit. 'MC' stands for multi-colour.

As the yarn in feeder 'B' is so thin, when the needles at the very edge are selecting it, the edge gets uneven. To avoid that, manually deselect 2 or 3 needles at the edge by pushing them all the way to the back. This way, those needles will knit with yarn in feeder 'A' instead and the edges will be even.

The needles that are brought forward will knit with the yarn in feeder B, the rest of the needles will knit with the yarn in feeder A. For this sample, I used a slightly tighter tension than I would normally for this yarn, as the stitches have the tendency to loosen up when the second yarn is so fine. This is just my preference.

A simpler way to create a see-through or sheer fabric is by knitting stockinette stitch using a very fine yarn. Just make sure to adjust the tension according to the yarn you are using, unless you prefer the look of looser stitches in the fine yarn. To create even more beautiful fabrics, combine that with a chunkier yarn to produce stripes alternating from fine to chunky.

You can create lovely fabrics even by simply combining stitches of mixed sizes by increasing and decreasing the tension used when knitting stockinette stitch. There are so many possibilities! I hope that this chapter has inspired you to spend some time developing lace samples and experimenting with yarn.

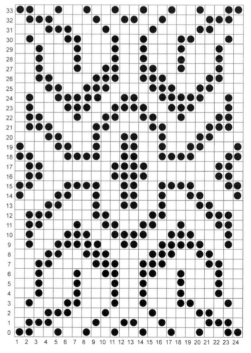

Punch-card chart. Every circle represents a square that must be punched on the card.

For this swatch I used a nylon yarn as the fine yarn and 2 ends of polyester viscose blend, 6000Nm as the chunky yarn.

CHAPTER 6

COMPLETE YOUR FIRST PROJECT

As a beginner it can be a little bit intimidating to machine knit your first garment. In this chapter I will show you, step-by-step, how to make your first accessory or jumper using some of the designs and techniques we have explored throughout the book. Starting with a simpler project is a great way to practise and develop your skills and make something for yourself that you can proudly wear.

The projects shown next should serve as examples and help guide you in making something for yourself or a friend using your own gauge and calculation.

PROJECT 1: LONG-STITCH SCARF

A scarf can be an easy first project; all you must do is decide how long and wide you wish your scarf to be, learn your gauge and translate the measurements to stitches and rows. It can easily become a statement piece when combining different techniques and yarns which is exactly what I did for the following scarf, and I love it. I used 2 yarns for this project, one on the cone which I will refer to as Yarn A, an alpaca, wool, and polyamide blend (count Nm 4000). Yarn B is a hand-knitting 4 ply yarn, 100 per cent cotton which I will use for the long-stitch rows.

Step 1: Calculating the gauge

You have learnt a couple of methods of calculating the gauge depending on your design: by counting stitches and rows or working the other way around and measuring your tension swatch first. For this scarf, I am combining long stitches and simple transfers and use both these methods to help me learn my gauge and keep track of my rows.

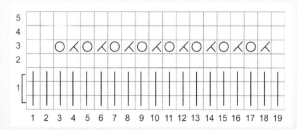

This is the chart of one repeat; row 1 is a long-stitch row, the rest knitted with the carriage while also producing eyelets using a 1-prong tool on row 3.

...continued on next page

…continued from previous page

This is my tension swatch. I cast on 30 stitches and its width measures 14.5cm. After calculating this, I decided to cast on double (60 stitches), so that my scarf is about 30cm wide.

I completed 6 repeats, and my swatch is 13.5cm long. One repeat consists of one long-stitch row knitted manually and 4 rows knitted with the carriage whilst executing transfers.

I could have also calculated 30 ÷ 14.5 = 2.06 to learn how many stitches per 1cm and use that to find out how many stitches I need to cast on so that my width is 30cm. That would have been 61.8 which I would usually round up to 62; however, I decided to have 61 stitches instead so that I have 2 stitches on both edges before the first and last eyelet. This will result in even and straight edges.

The length I wanted this scarf is to be is about 200cm, as I personally prefer to wear longer scarves. I know that if I complete 6 repeats 10 times, the length will be about 135cm which means that I must complete 6 repeats 15 times so that the total length is 200cm.

When knitting long stitches, in order to keep track of how many repeats I complete, I usually like to write the total number of repeats on a piece of paper and draw a tick mark next to them as soon as I complete them. This method might be the best option for some of the long-stitch designs, especially when you are not knitting any rows with the carriage. When planning this scarf, I realised that I could use the row counter to help me keep track of the rows instead.

I know that I must do 6 repeats 15 times; every time I complete 6 repeats, I will manually knit 6 long-stitch rows and 24 rows with the carriage. Only the rows knitted with the carriage will trip the row counter and I can calculate 24 × 15 = 360. That gives me the total number of rows I must knit so that my scarf is 200cm.

Knit your tension swatch and use the same calculation basis to learn your gauge and plan a scarf of your desired size.

Step 2: Knitting

The ball of yarn I used for the long-stitch rows is placed on the floor. It is best to unwind some yarn from the ball so that there is no resistance when knitting the stitch.

After completing the long-stitch row, I pulled the needles all the way out and knitted the first row with the carriage using yarn A.

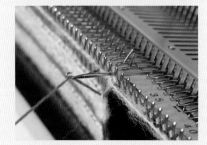

To carry up yarn B and avoid getting large loops and uneven edges, I took the end and manually knitted a stitch with the last needle.

After knitting the second row in yarn A, I transferred every other needle to the right to form an eyelet, placed all needles back in action and knitted 2 more rows.

Again, I manually knitted a stitch at the edge to carry up yarn B. I have now completed one repeat; to start a new repeat I must continue with another long-stitch row.

To make sure that I pinned it to the correct width, I used my measuring tape to guide me when pinning the other side.

Step 3: Blocking

If you do not have enough blocking matts to create a long and wide enough surface to block your scarf, using towels or some sheets works fine as well.

I used 2 clean sheets and folded them so that I have a soft layer in which I can place the pins. I first pinned one edge as straight as possible.

Step 4: Finishing touch

I love knitting scarfs as they are very easy; the part that I find a bit trickier sometimes is making sure that they look professionally finished. Ideally, I would not want my edges to be uneven or to curl too much, and the best way to help with that is by wet blocking the fabric (as demonstrated in Chapter 1). It will depend, however, on the yarn and technique used. In some instances, this technique does not stop the curling and I need to resort to more creative methods. One of my favourite ways to resolve the issue and simultaneously add a little extra detail is to do a couple of rows of crochet around the edges.

As the edges of this scarf are not curling as much and I am happy with how they look, I decided to simply add a little detail and a bit of weight to it by adding fringes on the ends.

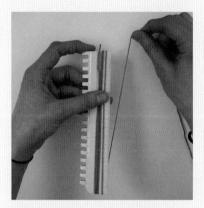

1. Wrap the yarn around a needle pusher 4 times; you may use a different object. The needle pusher is about 16cm so the fringes will end up being about 8cm long.

2. Snap the yarn and remove it from around the needle pusher. I like to have a few fringes prepared to be attached to the scarf.

3. Place a latch tool or crochet hook through an eyelet; I will go through the knit side of the fabric as I am considering this to be the wrong side.

4. Fold a fringe as evenly as possible in half and hold it that way as you pull it through the hole.

5. Once you have pulled the fringe, hold it to pull it again through the loop formed. It will make it easier to pull if you hold it closer to the end of the fringe like so.

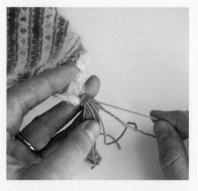

6. Bring all the ends through the hole and try to tighten it as neatly as possible. You can always pull a specific end to even out the knot if needed.

7. Cut the folded ends of the fringe as shown; do not worry if they are not all equal, you can even them out at the end.

Fringes attached to the scarf. Having the eyelets makes the process easier as we know exactly where to place the fringes and they are evenly spaced.

Finished project.

PROJECT 2: SCRUNCHIE

The second project is a scrunchie. This is also a great opportunity to empty cones that do not have enough yarn for a bigger project. I plied up 2 yarns for this project. One end of 2/28 Nm, 100 per cent cashmere and one end of wool-nylon blend, 1/15 Nm. The yarns were placed together through the yarn tension unit.

Step 1: Calculating the gauge

From my tension swatch I have learnt that I have 25 stitches and 32 rows per 10cm. I want my scrunchie to be 60cm long and 12cm wide, unfolded. You can choose different measurements, depending on the look you would like to achieve. Next, you can see how to apply your gauge and convert cm to stitches and rows.

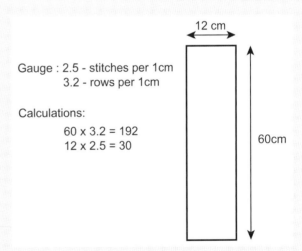

Gauge : 2.5 - stitches per 1cm
3.2 - rows per 1cm

Calculations:
60 x 3.2 = 192
12 x 2.5 = 30

This is how I like to plan simple designs; I will draw the shape I want to create and write all the measurements and calculations. For the scrunchie, I know that I must cast on 30 stitches and knit 192 rows.

...continued on next page

...continued from previous page

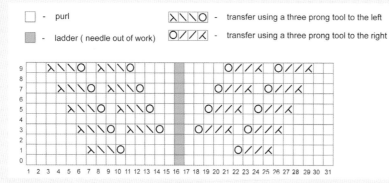

This is the chart for the stitch repeat. I accommodated the number of rows and stitches to make sure that the repeat is continuous and spaced evenly, so I cast on 31 stitches and knitted 200 rows.

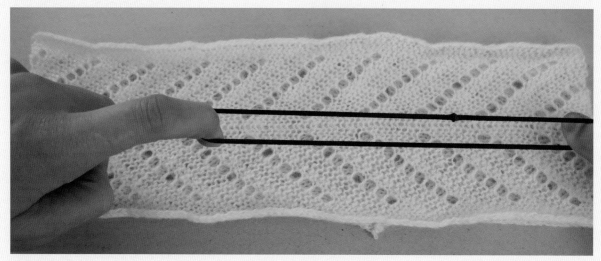

When planning your scrunchie make sure that you measure the elastic you want to use when it is fully stretched. The loop you will create from your rectangle of knitted fabric must be wider than that, so you do not lose the elasticity.

Step 2: Knitting

I did a quick waste yarn cast-on, knitted a few rows in waste yarn, threaded my main yarn and e-wrapped to cast on. After knitting the first row I transferred to form the ladder and after row 2, I began transferring stitches to form eyelets, as per the chart.

While knitting the scrunchie, I made a couple of mistakes such as forgetting to put the needle back in action or missing a transfer altogether; I will show you how you can fix these mistakes if they should happen. This is one of the reasons I love knitting so much – most of the time I can go back a few rows and fix any mistakes I've made.

If you forget to produce an eyelet altogether and realise this after you have knitted the 2 rows, you can go back and fix that without unravelling the entire 2 rows. You can unravel a few rows to fix a multitude of mistakes, but it is best not go back for too many rows as this can cause stitches to drop and make the situation even worse. It is a good idea to try and fix mistakes even when you are testing, just to practise this useful skill.

Before knitting the last row and casting off, I held the purl bar of an adjacent stitch to stop the ladder from forming. I did wash and block the scrunchie so that the cashmere could become softer and fluffier. Depending on the yarn you are using, you might consider washing and blocking your fabric as well, but don't worry about edges rolling as once sewn together, they will not curl anymore.

If you forgot to place the needle back in action before knitting the 2 rows, you can easily fix it by taking the 2 floats that were formed and hooking them back on the needle. Push the needle out, leave the first float on the needle, then place the second float on the open hook and push the needle back to complete the stitch.

These eyelets are created using a 3-prong tool so you must unravel 4 stitches, 2 rows back. Hold the 2 floats out of the way and transfer the stitches to create the eyelet that was missed, while not removing the weights from the sample.

Push the 4 needles out and, one at a time, manually knit the stitches starting at one side and keeping an even tension. You must complete 2 rows, so make sure the floats belong to the correct row when you are knitting.

Step 3: Putting the scrunchie together

STEP-BY-STEP: MAKING THE SCRUNCHIE

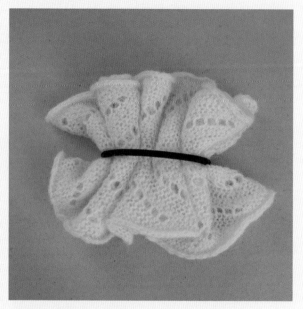

1. Stitch by stitch, sew together the ends of your knitted piece and create a tube. Use a darning needle and sew on the right side of the fabric.

2. Turn the fabric so that the purl or wrong side is facing you, gather it together as shown and wrap the elastic around it.

3. Find the first seams and fold the fabric to trap the elastic inside. This will be the starting point to sew the edges.

4. Sew the edges together with the right side facing you by catching the bars that run between the first and second stitch.

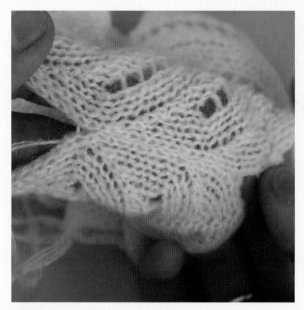

5. This method of sewing edges together is called a mattress stitch and the result will always be neat.

Finished project.

PROJECT 3: MITTENS

The third project is a pair of mittens, which you can adapt to the desired size and incorporate any design you wish. I have used 2 ends of 2/14 Nm, 100 per cent lambswool to make these mittens and they came out extremely soft and cosy.

You will need a ribber bed to create the ribbing but if you have a single bed only, you can produce ribbing manually or use other techniques. Planning and testing is key for this project; be prepared to knit a couple of samples before you make a mitten which fits perfectly. Making more than one sample is often part of the process in producing knitwear and it is always a learning opportunity.

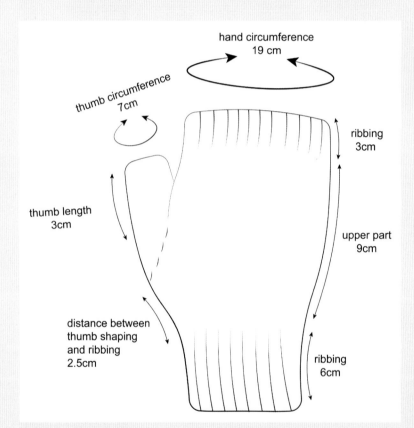

This is the sketch of the mitten; I wrote down all the measurements taken from my hand. Draw this on a piece of paper and write your own measurements.

Step 1: Calculate the gauge

Knit a tension swatch and count how many stitches and how many rows per 10cm². Make sure to wash and dry the fabric before counting. Lambswool, for example, shrinks a little bit when washed, so if you count stitches from an unwashed swatch your finished product might come out too small. It is also a good idea to knit some ribbing. I used a 1×1 rib, but you can use a different size if you prefer.

My gauge is 26 stitches per 10cm and 39 rows per 10cm, which means that I have 2.6 stitches and 3.9 rows per 1cm.

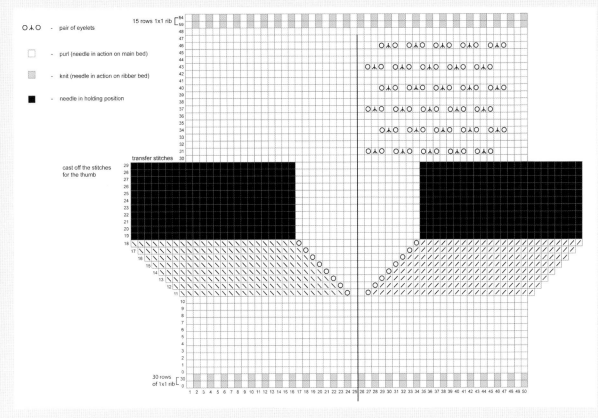

After converting all those measurements to stitches and rows, I was able to create a chart. Having a chart can be very useful, especially when you have a more intricate pattern.

Step 2: Knitting

Cast on 50 stitches and knit 30 rows of 1×1 ribbing then transfer all stitches from ribber bed to main bed. I knitted the cast-on row followed by 3 rows tubular on the tightest tension and the remaining rib on tension 3. The body was knitted on tension 8. I am sharing the tension in case you are using the same yarn.

After transferring all stitches to the main bed, remove all the weights and leave the cast-on comb only. In addition, you need to return the row counter to zero and then knit 10 rows.

…continued on next page

...continued from previous page

Using a 5-prong tool and starting from the edge, transfer stitches across in multiple steps until emptying a needle in the very centre.

Repeat the same on the other side; when finished, you will have 2 stitches with one out of action on both sides and the sample will be increased by 2 stitches.

Repeat the process until you have increased by as many stitches as you need and knit one row in between. I must increase by 18 stitches in total, taking my sample from 50 to 68 stitches.

Put half the number of needles you began with in holding position; I will put 25 on the opposite side where the carriage is. The carriage is also in holding position.

Knit one short row, place the same number of needles on hold on the other side. Attach a couple of claw weights to create tension for the stitches remaining in working position.

Knit as many rows as you want for the thumb and move the claw weights up every few rows as you knit. I knitted 11 rows and began casting off.

Remove the fabric and transfer stitches back to the centre or the initial needle formation. We now have 50 needles in action, just as we had at the beginning.

You can now begin the lace pattern; you could begin the pattern from the very beginning if you wish. If you choose to do that, you must make sure to first transfer stitches across to increase, and then produce the design, as it can be quite difficult to transfer if a needle has more than one stitch. Also, the tension created when increasing so many stitches every one row might make that process a bit more difficult. Testing what works is very important.

I transferred stitches and produced eyelets every 3 rows as per the chart. I only want the design to be visible on the outer side of the mitten, so I must create eyelets on one half only. I will mirror it for the other mitten.

I continued the lace pattern for 18 rows, finishing by knitting 15 rows of 1×1 rib. Here, I am casting off using the chain stitch method as I prefer the outcome. To do that, knit the last row at a looser tension.

Step 3: Putting the mittens together

Putting the mittens together is very easy as we only have 2 seams to do, one to close off the thumb while the other closes the exterior side of the mitten. I did

not wet block these mittens as the rib stopped the edges from rolling; the thumb edge did not curl either after sewing it together. I decided to do the seam, tie in the ends, wash and let it dry flat on a towel.

Using a mattress stitch will give you a perfect finish and the illusion that there is no seam. You can leave longer tails when you snap your yarn at the end and use them to sew the sides together. This way you will have less ends to tie in when finished.

The process

I knitted 3 samples in total before reaching the desired result. The first sample knitted enabled me to get familiar with the technique. Once I had learnt it, I was able to use my gauge and begin developing the mitten.

Therefore, the third sample is the one I was happy with. I hope this gives you an insight on the process of a knitting project. Give it a try, following the chart shown earlier to practise and then develop it further if needed according to your measurements.

This is the second sample; this time, I have knitted the top part one side at a time using partial knitting (just as we did for the thumb). Only after knitting this sample, I got the idea to transfer the stitches after completing the thumb and knit the rest in one go to avoid having a second seam.

Finished project.

PROJECT 4: DROPPED-SLEEVE JUMPER

The last project is a dropped-sleeve jumper with a wide neckline and rib lace detail. This is a very easy jumper to make as the style of neckline chosen does not require any shaping; only the sleeves are shaped which are simple to calculate and knit. Hopefully you can adapt the step-by-step instructions to make a similar version in your preferred style. You can use any lace designs covered in the book to make this jumper and can adjust the measurements to the fit you would like to achieve; this style is cropped but you can adapt this to your liking.

The yarn I used for this project is one end of 2/28 Nm cashmere and one end of 2/14 Nm lambswool in beige and cream; using 2 yarns of slightly different tones will produce a marbly effect. For the stripe detail I used a cotton acrylic blend fancy yarn, which is made from one end bouclé, one slub.

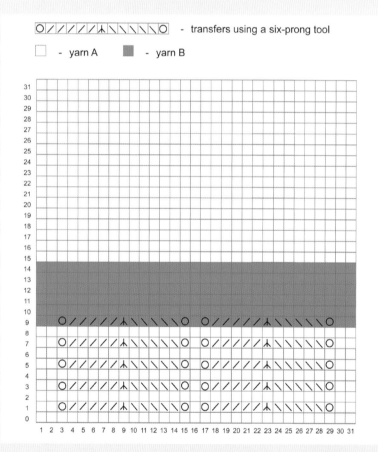

This is the chart for the lace stitch repeat; a repeat is over 14 stitches. If you would like the stripes to have more of a zigzag effect, knit less rows after doing the transfers.

Charts for the ribbing stitch; For the body I knitted 6 rows before and after the stitch repeat, for the sleeve I knitted 16. Adding more rows makes the cuff a little tighter.

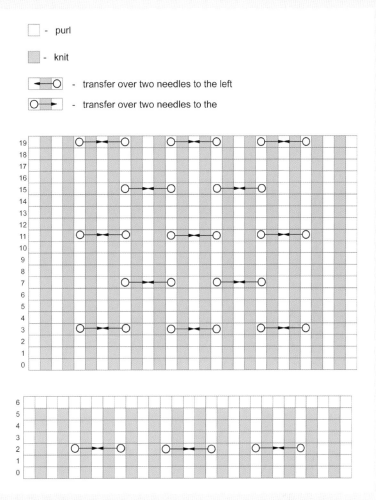

☐ - purl

▨ - knit

◄──O - transfer over two needles to the left

O──► - transfer over two needles to the

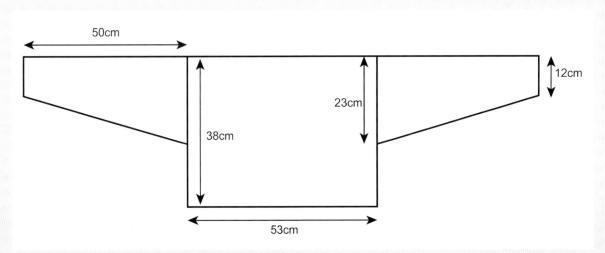

A flat drawing of the jumper with all the measurements in centimetres, including the ribbing. If you are not sure how to begin planning, you can always measure a jumper you like the fit of.

Step 1: Calculate the gauge

Knit a tension swatch, wash it, and count how many stitches and how many rows per 10 cm². My gauge for the body is 28 stitches and 45 rows, which means I have 2.8 stitches and 4.5 rows per 1cm.

Step 2: Knitting

The front and back panels

The front and back panels of this jumper are quite straightforward to knit as they are just 2 rectangles. Once I decided that the rib is 5cm, I subtracted that from the initial measurement and calculated using my gauge as follows:

Calculations for the front and back panels:

$$53 \times 2.8 = 148.4$$
$$33 \times 4.5 = 148.5$$

To knit the front and back panels of my jumper, I must cast on 149 stitches and knit 148 rows. Use your gauge to calculate in the same way according to your measurements. I rounded the number of stitches up as I have an odd number repeat for the stitch. When I have an odd number repeat, I always begin with the specific stitch in the very middle to ensure that my pattern is perfectly centred.

If you would also like to add stripes, divide the number of rows you must knit and include them where you wish to have them. Writing the plan on a piece of paper is very useful to know exactly the row number where you must change the yarn and so forth.

When I knitted the ribbing, I increased the tension slightly for the sections with transfers to not risk breaking the yarn and returned it back to the tighter one for the plain rows.

The sleeve panel

You can choose not to shape the sleeve either if you would like it to be straight and have a wider cuff. This is a dropped shoulder sleeve which means that the armhole position falls on top of the arm and not

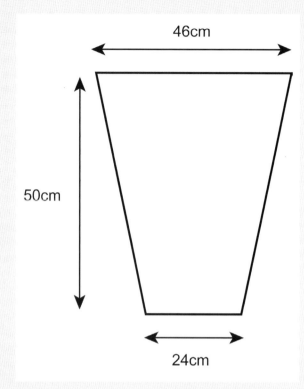

This is the flat drawing of the sleeve with all the measurements in centimetres. The sleeve width is narrower at the bottom and wider at the top, meaning that I must increase to shape it.

on top of the shoulder point (as it would sit for a set-in sleeve). Next, you will see all the calculations I did to knit the sleeve; you can use the same 'formula', replace it with your numbers and plan the sleeve of your jumper.

Calculations for the sleeve:

$$24 \times 2.8 = 67.2 \text{ (rounded up to 68)}$$
$$46 \times 2.8 = 128.8 \text{ (rounded down to 128)}$$

The depth of the cuff is 10cm, which leaves me with 40cm to knit.

$$40 \times 4.5 = 180$$

I now know that I must cast on 68 and increase to 128 stitches in 180 rows. There are 60 stitches to be increased or 30 pairs (as we are shaping both edges).

RIGHT: I transferred using a 3-prong tool to increase and left the needle I emptied out of action to produce an eyelet along the fashioning. This will add a little detail on the sleeve seam.

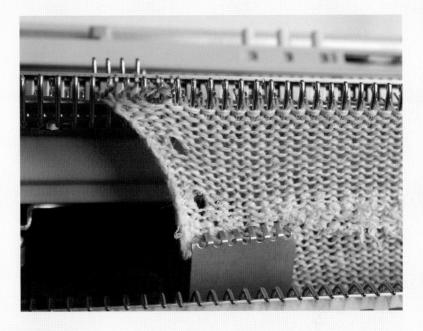

BELOW: All the panels flat on the floor. At this stage they are only steamed; the next step is to remove the waste yarn and sew the panels together. I will do it by hand, but you can use a linker if you have one.

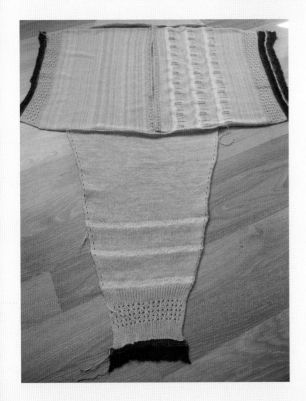

The increases must happen within the 180 rows we must knit; we can now calculate how to evenly distribute the increases:

$$180 \div 30 = 6 -$$

This means I must increase one stitch on each side every 6 rows.

Often, the result of this calculation is a non-integer number. If, for example, I have to knit 160 rows and increase the same number of stitches, the calculation would be $160 \div 30 = 5.3$. In this case I would increase every 5 rows until row 150, then knit the remaining 10 rows straight at the top of the sleeve.

When casting off the sleeve, before taking it off the machine, you can use a contrast yarn and mark the centre of the top of the sleeve. This will serve as a guide when sewing the sleeve to the body.

Step 3: Sewing the jumper

To put the jumper together, we must complete 4 seams: the shoulder seam, one attaching the sleeve to the body, followed by the underarm and side seams.

To finish the jumper, I have sewn in all the ends, washed it gently by hand and let it dry flat on a towel. You can choose to block your panels individually before sewing them together instead; it really depends on what design you use.

The top ribbing will be joined on the shoulder which will add a nice detail to the jumper. You can pin the front and back panels together first to decide how wide you would like the shoulder seam and neck opening to be, depending on the fit you would like to achieve.

To attach the sleeves to the body, align the mark you made with the shoulder seam. Measure and pin on the front and back panels up to where the sleeve should be sewn on. I know that my sleeve is 46cm at the top, so I will mark 23cm from the shoulder seam on both panels.

The next seams are the underarm and side seams. Begin from the rib to ensure that it is nice and straight, then continue sewing up. I used a mattress stitch to achieve a neat seam. Here, you may notice the eyelets I created when I increased without using the purl bar to form a stitch.

Finished project.

INDEX

First published in 2023 by
The Crowood Press Ltd
Ramsbury, Marlborough
Wiltshire SN8 2HR

enquiries@crowood.com
www.crowood.com

British Library Cataloguing-in-Publication Data
A catalogue record for this book is available from the
British Library.

ISBN 978 0 7198 4303 7

Cover design by Sergey Tsvetkov

Typeset by SJmagic DESIGN SERVICES, India
Printed and bound in India by Parksons Graphics Pvt. Ltd.

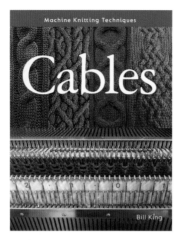

ISBN: 978 0 71984 193 4

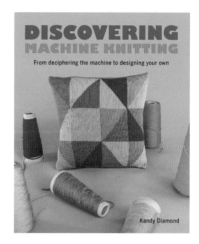

ISBN: 978 0 71984 199 6

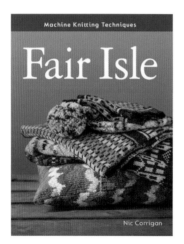

ISBN: 978 0 71984 157 6

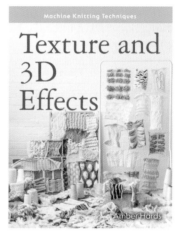

ISBN: 978 0 71984 238 2

ISBN: 978 0 71984 189 7